How to Win *Sales* & Influence *Spiders*

Boosting Your
Business & Buzz
on the Web

Catherine Seda

New Riders

VOICES THAT MATTER™

How to Win Sales & Influence Spiders: Building Your Business & Buzz on the Web
Catherine Seda

New Riders

1249 Eighth Street
Berkeley, CA 94710
510/524-2178
800/283-9444
510/524-2221 (fax)

Find us on the Web at: www.newriders.com
To report errors, please send a note to errata@peachpit.com
New Riders is an imprint of Peachpit, a division of Pearson Education
Copyright © 2007 by Catherine Seda

Project Editor: Michael J. Nolan
Development/Copy Editor: Marta Justak
Production Editor: Tracey Croom
Proofreader: Liz Welch
Compositor: Jerry Ballew
Indexer: Cheryl Landes
Cover design: Mimi Heft, Andreas Schueller
Interior design: Mimi Heft

ISBN 0-321-49659-0

9 8 7 6 5 4 3 2 1

Printed and bound in the United States of America

Foreword

The advent of the Web has been both a blessing and a curse for most entrepreneurs. The upside is obvious—millions of potential customers. The downside? Thousands of other sites selling similar products. So how do you stand up to the increased competition? Marketing, of course. Marketing has always been the key to success for many entrepreneurs; the best product (or service) in the world will remain on the shelf if no one knows it exists.

In today's more crowded marketplace, marketing is even more crucial to business success. Whether you already own your own business, are planning to start one, or have marketing responsibilities in someone else's company, you must have an effective marketing plan to survive. To do more than that—to thrive— that marketing strategy must include a strong Internet component. The new technologies may sound overwhelming, but it's essential you figure them out.

Take search, for example. Shoppers have always searched. Ten years ago, that meant heading to the mall and walking in and out of every store looking for the "perfect" item and hoping the seller had it in the right color or size. Depending on where your store was located, your marketing campaign might have included some local newspaper ads or radio spots. But chances are you did nothing and waited for customers to just drop in.

Today, ask shoppers if they search before buying, and you'll likely hear which search engine delivers the best results. Search engine optimization shouldn't be your only online strategy, but it's a critical one. And one that is supported by, not obstructed by, your other online marketing campaigns. Each Internet strategy must be optimized to achieve higher profits while also being optimized for the search engines.

Don't worry—luckily, you don't have to figure it all out on your own. Catherine Seda has done all the hard work for you. The first chapter alone on search engine optimization is worth the cost of this book.

In Chapter 2, Catherine tells you how she came to write a monthly column for us at *Entrepreneur* magazine. That just shows you she practices what she preaches. Catherine doesn't deal in theory. *How to Win Sales & Influence Spiders* is filled with the kind of information and insight that can only come from an insider, someone who's been on the leading edge of Internet marketing for the past decade.

In the nearly 25 years I've been involved with entrepreneurial businesses, I have never witnessed anything as powerful as the Internet. Harnessing the Web has given us the power to transform and revolutionize not only our businesses, but also the way we conduct business. By guiding you through the Internet's most powerful marketing strategies, Catherine Seda will help you do just that.

Rieva Lesonsky
Editorial Director
Entrepreneur® magazine

Table of Contents

Acknowledgements

This book was a lot tougher to write than my first book, *Search Engine Advertising* (New Riders, 2004). I wrote *How to Win Sales & Influence Spiders* in a few months and then spent almost a year rewriting it…over and over again. Thankfully, I had a great team cheering me on.

First, I'm grateful to New Riders for again believing in my vision. It's an honor to work with your fun, creative, and supportive team! Nancy Aldrich-Ruenzel and Nancy Davis, thank you for publishing two books of mine and for everything your team does behind the scenes to make this happen. Michael Nolan, thank you for getting me on board and being excited about this project. Marta Justak, I value your support, insight, and dedication to creating a book I can be proud of. Tracey Croom, I appreciate your attention to production details. Mimi Heft and Andreas Schueller, I love my cover. Glenn Bisignani, your marketing efforts are much appreciated.

Thank you Chris Sherman for editing my book on planes, in cars, and while working around the world. Amanda Watlington, I really appreciate your valuable contributions to my chapter on social media. Rieva Lesonsky, thank you for your foreword.

Bryan Eisenberg, David McInnis, and Mike Drew let me bounce book title ideas off their heads. Thanks guys! Bryan, your subtitle is perfect—it stayed.

A big "thank you" goes to my colleagues who share their insider tips in this book: John Battelle, Alexandria Brown, Declan Dunn, Janelle Elms, Cliff Ennico, David Johnson, Andrew Goodman, David McInnis, Chris Sherman, Nick Usborne, Dr. Amanda Watlington, and Jeremy Wright.

And I'm equally grateful to the companies that let me share their successes: Beachcombers Bazaar, Custom Direct, Entrepreneur Media, Everywhere Marketing, Fire Mountain Gems and Beads, Larry Star, Nixon, Paradise Ranch Country Club for Dogs, Park City Mountain Resort, Viewstream, WebTrends, and the World Wildlife Fund.

Pete Nelson, Ann Convery, Lorrie Morgan-Ferrero, Christine Kloser, and Jen Seda, you inspire me. Janet Anderton, you keep me sane.

I'm giving a special shout-out to my friends who heard me say too many times "Can't talk now; I'm writing." Annie, Brooke, Bunny, Cindy, David, Kali, Lan, Lee, Lesley, and Sara—I'm ready to play! Mom, is it spa time again?

And finally, I thank you for reading. Hoping something I say helps your business is the reason why I write.

About the Author

Catherine Seda

Catherine is a 12-year Internet marketing veteran, columnist for *Entrepreneur* magazine, and author of *Search Engine Advertising* (New Riders, 2004).

She teaches business professionals how to attract new customers, search engine spiders, and the press simultaneously. Her unique approach enables entrepreneurs to increase their business by up to $100,000 in 30 days. Corporate marketers can increase their business by $1 million a month or more.

As a popular speaker, Catherine shares practical Internet marketing tips at leading educational institutions and industry conferences such as eBay Live!, eBay University, Search Engine Strategies, The DMA Catalog Conference, and UC San Diego Extension. She is currently Dean of Internet Marketing at LA College International.

In addition to being *Entrepreneur* magazine's "Net Sales" columnist, Catherine writes articles for publications such as eBay magazine, Leader magazine, Search Engine Watch, Yahoo! Small Business Insights, and the U.S. Small Business Administration's Small Business Success. She is also frequently quoted in eWeek.com, CNET news.com, eBay Radio, American Public Media's Marketplace, and other news outlets.

Catherine loves Internet marketing because she loves speed. In fact, she survived skeleton training at the Utah Olympic Park during which she raced down an icy bobsled track, head-first, on a sled, at 70 MPH. For companies looking to bring speed and power to their Internet marketing performance, Catherine is the perfect match.

To get Catherine's free "Top 10 Internet Marketing Mistakes" report and more how-to tips, visit **www.CatherineSeda.com**.

Technical Editor

Chris Sherman

Chris Sherman is president of Searchwise LLC, a Boulder, Colorado-based Web consulting firm, and executive editor of SearchEngineLand.com. Chris is also chair and organizer of Incisive Media's international Search Engine Strategies conferences.

Chris has written about search and search engines since 1994. His clients have included International Data Corporation, Accenture, Motorola, Levi-Strauss, Nokia, Ortho Biotech, Porsche, United Technologies, and the Scripps Clinic. From 1998 to 2001, he was the Web search guide for About.com. Chris holds a master's degree in Interactive Educational Technology from Stanford University and a bachelor's degree in Visual Arts and Communications from the University of California, San Diego.

Chris is a Web search university faculty member, and is an honorary inductee of the Internet Librarian Hall of Fame. He is the author of *Google Power: Unleash the Full Power of Google*, *The Invisible Web: Uncovering Information Sources Search Engines Can't See* (with Gary Price), *The McGraw-Hill CD ROM Handbook*, *The Elements of Basic*, *The Elements of Cobol*, and *The Elements of Pascal*.

He is frequently quoted in *The Wall Street Journal*, *The New York Times*, *Business Week*, *USA Today*, and other publications, and has appeared on CNN, NPR, CBS and other television and radio networks.

Chris has been unsuccessful in his attempts to persuade Stanford to strip his degree so he can join the founders of Yahoo! and Google in boasting about *not* graduating from the university.

Contributing Author

Amanda G. Watlington, Ph.D., APR

Amanda is the founder of Searching for Profit, a search marketing strategy consultancy. Prior to founding Searching for Profit, Amanda was director of research for a leading Search Engine Optimization firm, assistant professor of Business at a midwestern college, and held leadership positions in marketing strategy, public relations, and healthcare publishing.

Amanda's creativity and expertise enabled her to develop patented language-based analytic tools and methodologies to support search engine marketing campaigns. She is a renowned expert on query behavior, query construction, and "the psychology of search."

As an internationally recognized speaker, she has led sessions on search marketing, Web strategy, and social media at Search Engine Strategies, WebmasterWorld, AdTech, DMA, and AIM's Net.Marketing conferences. She's the author of three books and has written feature articles for over 30 magazines and journals. Her most recent book entitled: *Business Blogs: A Practical Guide* was published in May 2005.

Intro

Wow!
Internet marketing is an entirely different game today, compared to the mid 1990s when I jumped in. It's a lot more complex, yet there are also new ways to reach customers—for free—using blogs and podcasts, for example.

There are also better ways to use Internet marketing to get free traffic from the search engines and free publicity from the press, while attracting new customers. This is critical. Let the spiders and press take your message far beyond your existing customers. That's optimized marketing. And that's how to boost your business and buzz on the Web.

This book reveals how to use Internet marketing to attract three audiences at once: new customers, search engine spiders, and the press.

As a search marketer and journalist, I'll give you a window into these worlds so that you can get maximum impact from your Internet marketing…often within 90 days. The speed of Internet success is addicting.

I love speed.

After writing my first book, *Search Engine Advertising*, I enrolled in the ultimate adrenaline adventure—skeleton school. In case you missed the winter Olympics, skeleton is a sport for insane people who race head-first on a sled down an icy bobsled track through hairpin turns at over 70 mph. During my training, several sliders suffered concussions, facial stitches, cracked ribs, chipped teeth, and ice burns. I escaped with a whiplash.

You know, Internet marketing is like skeleton. It's an exhilarating ride, only it's far less dangerous to your health. If you're looking to bring speed and power to your Internet marketing campaigns, this book is for you.

Who Should Read This Book?

I wrote *How to Win Sales & Influence Spiders* for business professionals who want to maximize their performance from Internet marketing...*fast*. You can achieve profitable results within 90 days, just like the consultants and companies featured in each chapter's "Success Story." Of course, you might achieve explosive success within 24-48 hours, too. This is a tactical book for "non-techies," including consultants, entrepreneurs, corporate marketers, students, investors, journalists, and adventurers.

How This Book Is Organized

I've organized this book into two parts: online public relations and online advertising.

Part I: Using Online Public Relations for Long-Term Success

PR is your storyteller. If told right, your story has "sticking power" on the Web. That's powerful. When your story comes from a third party, you're legitimized as a credible source. You then achieve expert status, which gives you the competitive edge online. In this section of the book, I cover search engine optimization, leveraging articles, blogging, social media, and broadcasting your message through Internet radio, podcasts, and webinars.

Part II: Making Online Advertising Profitable for Your Business

Advertising is your sales rep. If sold right, your ad persuades customers to "buy now" or at least opt in to your community. Reach the "right" audience and deliver the "right" message, and you'll catapult your revenue and profits. Online advertising has challenges for attracting spiders and journalists. Not to worry. The seemingly impossible can be done. In this section of the book, I discuss e-mail marketing, affiliate marketing, pay-per-click, contextual advertising, and shopping communities.

What This Book Doesn't Cover

This is *not* a technical step-by-step book. This book *does* cover key tactics, practical tips, and success stories you can use immediately…or when you're ready, even as technology continues to evolve. And I share my personal experiences on what works, what doesn't, and how to avoid falling into potholes.

For links to the tools I discuss in my book, and more how-to tips, visit my Web site at **www.CatherineSeda.com**. Got an Internet marketing question or a success story? Send me an e-mail or post a comment on my blog. I'm always looking for information to share with my fellow entrepreneurs.

To your online success!

Catherine Seda
Internet & Search Marketing Strategist
Entrepreneur Columnist
www.CatherineSeda.com

I

Using Public Relations for Long-Term Success

1
Winning the SEO Battle

Search engine marketing is on fire. It's still one of the most cost-effective ways for businesses to attract new customers online. Unfortunately, it's become a fierce fight among marketers battling to maintain top positions while squeezing higher profits from their campaigns. Attracting profitable customers isn't the only benefit of getting top positions, however.

Many members of the media start their research with a keyword search. Companies at the top get the interview. Those that lack search engine visibility miss connecting with the press, as well as prospects.

For these reasons, understanding search engine optimization is key to everything else you do online. As a search marketing insider for over 10 years, I've seen where the opportunities exist for achieving top visibility. As an *Entrepreneur* magazine columnist and freelance writer, I know that the media is watching. Connecting with customers online is only partial success.

To maximize the impact of the most powerful Internet marketing strategies, you must leverage the Web for three audiences simultaneously: new customers, search engine spiders, and the press.

What Is Search Engine Marketing?

Search engine marketing consists of two complementary but very different campaigns: *search engine optimization* (SEO) and *pay-per-click* (PPC). SEO falls into online public relations because many consumers see search engines as editorial gatekeepers, displaying "the best" matches for their searches. Ha! We know differently. We know that we can influence those rankings, and we do so, in every way possible. While most people consider SEO to be PR, pay-per-click is definitely thought of as online advertising. I'll talk more about PPC later in Chapter 8, but I want to focus on SEO now.

Through SEO, you can improve your Web page rankings in the organic search results (also called *natural search results*). Here's how it works. The search engines send out *spiders* (also called *crawlers*) to scour the Web and collect Web pages for the search engines' databases. Spiders build up a search engine's library of Web pages, so to speak. Many search engines such as Ask. com, Google, MSN Search, and Yahoo! display both paid and organic results on the same page.

SEO is a tedious and often frustrating process because top rankings are never guaranteed, and when achieved, they need constant protection from the search engines' ever-changing algorithms (a mathematical formula used to rank Web pages) and your competitors' continual optimization efforts. Is it worth it? You bet! Who wouldn't want free targeted traffic? The more clicks you get, the more profitable your campaign will be.

Admittedly, it's harder to get top organic rankings today than it was a few years ago. There are more Web pages vying for your keywords. Plus, because more companies are outsourcing their SEO strategy to professionals, it's become a case of SEO expert versus SEO expert. Is getting top rankings even possible? Yes. But now more than ever, you must start with a solid strategy, while avoiding problem practices or SEO professionals who spam their way to the top.

I'll reveal the dominant strategies you need to make your SEO campaign successful, whether you manage this in-house or through an outside vendor. Because SEO is a moving target, I won't go into great detail about today's technical tactics because they could be obsolete by the time you read this book. But I will get a bit techie in the spam sections because the tactics I cover aren't likely to stop being spam anytime soon.

Are you ready to attract fame, fortune, and fans? Then let's dive into search engine optimization by uncovering the first common problem area: your keyword strategy.

> ✦ *Tip:* Visit **www.CatherineSeda.com** *for free resources and updated links to cool tools.*

Think Theme

Because choosing keywords is the first step in search marketing, it's also the first place marketers make mistakes. Free tools such as Yahoo!'s Keyword Selector Tool, the Google AdWords keyword tools, and Good Keywords show you related keywords that could work for your business. WordTracker and KeywordDiscovery are subscription-based tools that can help you dig even deeper.

Not so fast! Simply getting keyword ideas and possibly an estimated volume of monthly searches for each keyword doesn't mean anything if you don't understand the importance of creating a killer keyword theme. Your SEO success starts here.

You can't just plunk keywords into your home page copy, thinking you're done. You've got to create a keyword theme for your entire Web site. Then you must assign supporting keywords to the pages you want ranked. Each page you want ranked essentially must stand on its own merits. In SEO, it's Web page versus Web page. Yet, each page must tie back into your site's overall theme. That's because a meaty site with many related pages helps individual pages get ranked.

Establish Relevancy

Creating a keyword theme is crucial for establishing relevancy. Relevancy is the #1 rule in SEO. Without it, techniques you use will either be ineffective or could be considered spam.

Here is an example of how to create a keyword theme. Say you're marketing gift baskets. Your primary product categories include baby gift baskets, birthday gift baskets, and holiday gift baskets. **Figure 1.1** shows a possible theme for the home page and three top-level category pages.

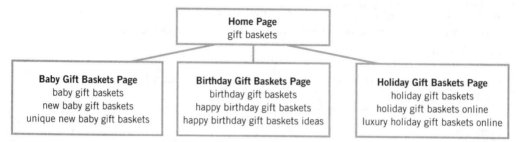

Figure 1.1   Creating a keyword theme.

See how each category page has its own theme, yet supports the main "gift baskets" theme? Don't copy this model exactly because my repetitive use of the keyword phrase "gift baskets" is spammy. Excessive repetition of keywords on a page is a big no-no. I'm oversimplifying this example to demonstrate the concept of keyword theming.

Now that you understand how to do this for your own site, you'll be well ahead of your competitors who are using keywords without a clue.

Before we move on, look at the Baby Gift Baskets page in Figure 1.1. An effective way to avoid a spam penalty is to use a keyword phrase that includes several keywords in it. For example, these are three possible keywords you could optimize to get organic rankings for "baby gift baskets":

✦ Baby gift baskets

✦ New baby gift baskets

✦ Unique new baby gift baskets

Focus on the keyword "unique new baby gift baskets" for a minute. How many combinations of other keywords do you see within this one phrase? For starters, how about:

✦ Unique baby gift

✦ Unique baby gift baskets

✦ New baby gift

✦ New baby gift baskets

✦ Baby gift

✦ Baby gift baskets

✦ Baby baskets

If you add keywords in front of or behind your core keyword, you'll score rankings for additional keyword phrases without spamming! I'll discuss more about avoiding spam violations a little later on in this chapter.

Are you seeing how to "think theme?" This is a critical concept to understand. Yet, it's not widely discussed. Most of the resources on SEO discuss keyword tools or how to choose relevant keywords. Those are important points, too. However, creating a killer keyword strategy starts with creating a relevant keyword theme for your Web site.

Page Optimization

Now you can optimize your Web pages for your keywords. For starters, sprinkle keywords in the following places:

✦ **URL/File names**

   It's probably not a good idea to change your primary domain name at this point. If you redesign your site, you could keep your domain name and place keywords in your file names. For example, `www.company.com/babygiftbaskets.html`.

✦ **Meta tags**

   These include a meta title, meta description, and meta keywords. This information is placed in the HTML code of your site pages. The meta title and description often appear as your Web site's listing in the organic search results. Today, the meta keywords tag itself has no power; however, when used in conjunction with the meta title and meta description, it could help.

✦ **Heading**

   A page heading is a text headline that is separated from the rest of your page copy. It gets the attention of humans and spiders. Geek speak coming...headings are `<h1>` to `<h6>` tags.

✦ **Alternate text**

   This is text for an image that's put inside the HTML code. Instead of images, alternative text can be shown to people with text browsers, handheld devices, and screen readers for people with disabilities. Search engines see this text also.

+   **Page copy**

    You must have keywords in visible page copy to rank well. Generally speaking, more copy is better than less copy. A few sentences aren't enough. Write copy to help humans and spiders determine what the page is about.

I'm tempted to go into more detail, but I won't. There are way too many techniques to cover in one chapter of a book. Plus, there are no one-size-fits-all answers to the specific SEO questions that you want to ask. That's because each site has a different structure, is at a different level of SEO readiness, and is battling against different competitors. My goal is to tell you the chief strategies you need to know about.

Speaking of strategies, creating a keyword theme for your site will prepare you for developing site content that counts. Your content has a significant impact on your rankings.

Content Is King

The search engines love, love, love content. Because they can't understand images, they rely on content to determine what a Web page is about.

After you've identified the keyword theme for a page, you need to know how many times to use the keyword(s) assigned to it. Use keywords too many times, and you'll be busted for spamming. Don't use them enough, and you won't climb into the top rankings. It's a dilemma.

Keyword Density

This is where *keyword density* comes in. Keyword density is the relationship of a keyword phrase to the total number of words on a page. If there are 100 words on a page and seven of them are your keyword, then your keyword density is 7 percent.

This might surprise you, but there's no magic keyword density number.

You have to optimize your Web page based on your competitors' Web pages. If competing Web pages have an average keyword density of 2 percent and yours has 7 percent, your page could scream "SPAMMER OVER HERE!" to the search engines. Or, if the top ten pages have an average keyword density of 7 percent and yours is 2 percent, your page won't be seen as equal to your competitors. Aim to fit in. A little above is fine, but don't try to kill your competition, or you will kill your page's ranking potential.

Here's a warning about keyword density. Look at the Web pages you're going to analyze. Spammers are often in the top ten rankings. If you include their pages in your analysis, you could be optimizing your pages for death. In the section on "Avoiding the Spam Police," I'll teach you what *not* to do so you won't be unfairly penalized for a spam violation. Also, refer to those tactics when evaluating your competitors.

Don't stress out over keyword density. Use it as a general guideline because the top ten Web pages fluctuate anyway.

Keep in mind that the search engines aren't ultimately your most important audience—your prospects and the press are. If your keyword density makes your page copy distracting, annoying, or illogical to humans to read, it's definitely too high—no matter what your competitors are doing.

Create Content

E-commerce sites generally have a problem when it comes to content. They don't have any—or at least enough of it. These sites have copy on the home page, but the supporting site pages tend to have just product images and links to the shopping cart. Without enough content, a spider can't tell if a home page about "baskets" should rank for "gift baskets," "picnic baskets," or "bike baskets."

To make matters worse, a Web page with a very high link-to-copy ratio raises another problem. It could be misinterpreted as spam because link farms and Web rings tend to have this characteristic. Those sites have little or no content, just a lot of links to boost the link popularity score of sites they link to. (I'll cover link popularity in the next section.) My point is, if most of the words on your site pages are hyperlinks, that's bad. You need to add relevant content. Here are a few solutions:

✦ **Add content to your product category pages.** For example, add content to www.company.com/babygiftbaskets.html. This copy will tell spiders and humans what this category of products is all about. The links on this page can take them deeper into your site.

◆ **Create and optimize content-only pages and then put them at a top level of your site's structure.** For example, you could create **www.company. com/babygiftideas.html**, or put your Baby Gift Ideas page inside a directory that might look like **www.company.com/babygiftbaskets/**. Spiders don't crawl more than a few levels deep, which is why juicy content pages need to be at a top level. A page inside **www.company.com/products/ newproducts/baskets/baby/giftbaskets** won't likely be found by spiders.

◆ **Create a sitemap, which is a Web page that lists the URLs of key content pages within your site.** Put this page at a top level of your site (for example, **www.company.com/sitemap.html**). Spiders will find this page and then crawl the pages you link to. And humans will find this index useful, too.

◆ **Consider feeding individual products pages to comparison shopping engines.** I'll refer to these engines as shopping communities in this book, such as BizRate, NexTag, PriceGrabber.com, and Shopping. com. Product pages are usually too deep within a site to be found by spiders anyway.

> ◆ **Note:** *One of my e-commerce clients showed me how a much smaller competitor with a cheesy-looking Web site outranked hers. My client's product inventory was much bigger, and her Web site was beautifully designed. However, along with other differences, my client's competitor had significantly more content on both his home page and top-level pages. So, I proposed that one of my client's action items should be to write "how-to" articles for her site, in order to educate potential customers and act as search engine spider bait. She needed Web pages with copy to balance out her Web pages that had mostly product photos and links.*

Let me bring up an important point about creating content pages. As I already mentioned, make sure that your copy serves your human audience. An educational page will rank far better in the organic search results than one created just to trick the search engines.

And remember to write content to lead your prospects into action or to invite the press to contact you. When it comes down to it, a #1 ranking doesn't matter if it doesn't generate new business. Include links to other resources on your site and, of course, to relevant products or services. That's an effective landing page for SEO—one that ranks well, brings in new visitors, and persuades them to take action.

Creating a keyword theme and relevant content make your Web site ready to be crawled by the search engine spiders. These are two of the three most powerful strategies in SEO. Yet the third one might have the biggest impact on your rankings—and that would be "popularity." The search engines will reward your site for being popular.

Popularity Matters

One way search engines determine how to rank Web pages is through link popularity. This term refers to the quantity and quality of links pointing to your Web site. High link popularity suggests your site is an expert resource, worthy of higher rankings than other sites.

Link Building Steps

There are many ways to get good links. Here are four simple steps for getting started.

1. **Identify high-ranked sites.**

   Start with the keyword phrase you want to be ranked for most. Run a search for it in Ask.com, MSN Search, Google, and Yahoo!. Check out the pages at the top of the organic results. Skip direct competitors. Choose professional-looking sites or blogs that have good-quality content similar to yours in theme.

2. **Request an inbound link.**

   E-mail is usually the most efficient way of asking for a link. This provides an e-mail trail, too. Avoid writing a generic-sounding link request because your e-mail could be blocked by spam filters or deleted by recipients. Instead, personalize and customize your e-mail. Include reasons why the recipient should link to your Web site and how your Web site could serve their visitors.

3. **Hyperlink keywords in your description.**

   Ask for your company name and a description to be put on your link partners' sites. Here's the secret step: *Include your keyword in your description and hyperlink it to your site.* Why? Spiders follow links on the Web. Keywords linked to your site get associated with your site. This is one of the critical steps that many business professionals don't know about—hopefully, your competitors!

4. **Use relevant landing pages.**

   Think "keyword theme" for a minute. You'll want sites and blogs to link to the page you're optimizing. Don't link them all to the home page. Use the most relevant page instead.

Google's PageRank can help you choose your link partners. PageRank is Google's system for ranking a Web page based on the quantity and quality of Web pages that link to it. The scoring scale is 0 to 10, with 10 being the best. Basically, the higher a page's PageRank score, the more you want a link from it because Google likes it.

You can download Google's toolbar, visit a Web page, and mouseover the PageRank bar in the toolbar to reveal the score.

A higher PageRank score doesn't equal a higher ranking, but it's a pretty important vote from Google, which certainly helps. Just don't rely exclusively on a PageRank score because the toolbar's data isn't very reliable.

Top Five Bad Link Neighborhoods

A discussion about link popularity isn't complete without warning you about "bad neighborhoods." You should link to other sites because an authority site does (get more links in than out, however). And that's the site you want to emulate. Spiders like expert sites.

But a link to a bad neighborhood can hurt your rankings. A site that offers little or no content, just a ton of links, is bad. Remember, spiders value content and relevancy. So, a lack of those two qualities should tip you off. Here are the top five kinds of neighborhoods to steer clear of:

1. **Web rings**

   A Web ring is a group of Web pages that only link together. One page links to another, which links out to another.

2. **Link farms**

   A link farm consists of a group of Web pages that all link to each other. Most of the time, a link farm doesn't contain much content, only links.

3. **Free-for-all sites**

   A free-for-all site allows people to submit their URL to a link directory. These sites might collect your e-mail address for spamming purposes.

4. **Link-infested directories**

   A link-infested directory may be focused on a particular topic, but it contains little or no content, just a bunch of links. Directories generally accept new link submissions, if relevant to the directory. (The major search engine directories such as the Open Directory Project and Yahoo! Directory are fine, even beneficial.)

5. **Guestbooks**

   A guestbook might allow participants to include a link to their sites or an e-mail address. Some SEO spammers have created software programs to post links to thousands of guestbooks at a time.

Insider Insights: Chris Sherman

Chris Sherman is president of Searchwise LLC, a Boulder, Colorado–based Web consulting firm, and executive editor of SearchEngineWatch.com.

What's the #1 mistake marketers make with SEO?

Thinking it's "too hard" or "too expensive." Even basic blocking and tackling (good titles, copy, link campaign) can be enormously effective. And for many Web sites, once optimization has been done, it can pay dividends for years with minimal ongoing cost.

What's your favorite simple but powerful tip?

Leverage those title tags! No matter how sophisticated SEO becomes or how many changes the search engines make to their algorithms, a good title remains crucial—not just for good ranking, but as a powerful call to action for searchers that should compel people to click on the result link.

How has SEO helped your business?

Since I've been writing about SEO from the beginning, I've leveraged my knowledge into writing, speaking, and consulting engagements. Ironically, I do little SEO work on my own site—I don't have time!

Notice any commonalities here? Most of these bad neighborhoods don't offer content, just links. Although guestbooks have content, it's not the right kind. What's the #1 rule for SEO? You got it: relevancy. Because anyone can create or post to a guestbook, the content isn't often relevant to much of anything.

And, in case you're wondering, blog spamming isn't a good idea either. Because blog marketing can enhance your SEO efforts, in the past few years blog spamming has replaced guestbook spamming. Blogs are actually better targets for spammers than guestbooks because good blogs are content rich and topically relevant. Don't be afraid to participate in blogs. Just be careful. If you post your relevant comments and your URL or e-mail address on a few blogs, you should be fine.

All right, you now know the essentials of improving your link popularity while avoiding bad neighborhoods. Think about getting links to and from content-relevant, quality sites and you'll be on the right path. Ethical linking takes time, and it's worth it.

Unfortunately, there are more tactics that are serious spam violations. Make sure that you, your Webmaster, or the SEO professionals you're planning to hire don't use any of those tactics, which I'll cover in the next section. You don't want to be caught by the spam police. Not being in a top ranking isn't nearly as bad as not appearing in the displayed search results at all.

Avoiding the Spam Police

The scary thing is that some spam works—until you're caught.

Spammers who play on the dark side of search with "black hat" SEO techniques often buy up domains for a "churn-and-burn" strategy. They use spamming tactics to shoot to the top of organic results. They hope their rankings last long enough to make money as an affiliate, ad publisher, or SEO marketer.

When a spam domain is caught and banned by the search engines, it's been burned. Spammers focus on their other domains. The churn-and-burn approach is not a healthy move for business owners. You never want to mess with your primary domain like that.

I'm going to assume that you're interested in playing by "white hat" rules. I'm going to share the worst spam violations so you can make sure you, or your SEO team, don't accidentally do something dangerous.

Seven Spamming Sins

In addition to the link spamming tactics discussed in the previous section, here are a few totally "old school" tactics; if you're caught using them, not only will you be penalized by the search engine spam police, but you also might be laughed at. Nobody wants that.

Don't use the following tactics:

1. **Doorway pages**

   Also called *gateway pages, entry pages, hallway bridges, bridge pages,* or probably half a dozen other names, doorway pages are created for spiders, not visitors. In fact, they're often hidden from visitors and contain links into your Web site that search engines follow.

2. **Meta refresh tags and redirects**

   A meta refresh tag, which is placed inside the HTML code of a Web page, can be used to redirect people automatically from one page to another without requiring them to click a link. Sometimes, a redirect is necessary.

   For example, if you completely redesign your Web site and all of the URLs change, you'll want people who find your old URLs to be automatically redirected to your new URLs. But unfortunately, because spammers often optimize a page for high-traffic keywords and then use the meta refresh tag to send people to a completely irrelevant Web page, your site could be unfairly penalized if you use a meta refresh tag this way. So instead, use a server-side redirect, called "301" to tell the search engines the old URLs have been permanently changed to the new ones. Speak to your geeks, and they should set this up without causing you any pain whatsoever. Internet geeks are gods.

3. **Duplicate content**

   Putting the same, or even similar, content on different domain names is considered to be duplicate content. The search engines don't want sites with the same content polluting their organic results. A previous client of mine tried this, even though I told him not to. Remarkably, his primary domain was not penalized, but none of his duplicate pages were indexed, even though the spiders did come check them out.

4. **Information pages**

   Because surfers and spiders value content, a domain name used as a single information page doesn't provide value. Don't take the dozens of domains you bought, post one page of content on each of them, optimize each for a keyword, and then link them all back to your Web site. Spiders will smell spam.

5.   **Hidden text**

The search engines can easily spot keywords camouflaged into the Web page's background color, in hidden links, and anywhere else that would not be easily seen by visitors. (Meta tags are fine because visitors can view the source code.) And just because you catch your competitors using hidden text doesn't mean you should. If your competitors jumped off a cliff...well, you know the rest.

6.   **Tiny text**

Making text super tiny so that visitors can't really see it, but technically it's not hidden, doesn't cut it either. Tiny text is spam, so don't go there.

7.   **Keyword stuffing**

Keyword stuffing, also called *keyword loading* or *keyword spamming,* is the overuse of keywords. (Refer back to the section "Content Is King" for more details on proper optimization.) Here's a quick way to tell if you are keyword stuffing: If what you're writing doesn't read well to humans, you're stuffing. Think humans before spiders.

There are more SEO "dos" and "don'ts," but if I overwhelm you now, you might give up and not do anything I recommend in this book. Actually, hiring an SEO consultant or firm is a pretty good idea unless you, or your team, want to become an SEO warrior. Unfortunately, I hear from business owners who get burned by SEO firms all the time. However, business owners also need reasonable expectations if they don't want their SEO firm spamming. In the next section, I'll shed light on what you can, and can't, expect from a search engine optimization firm or consultant.

SEO Professionals: Snakes and Saints

Choosing an SEO consultant or firm is challenging. Unlike choosing a Web site designer, you can't really see what you're getting. Will search engine spammers tell you they spam? Not likely. But I have talked to a few spammers who admit and proudly say they do "black hat" SEO because that gets them clients looking for an instant traffic jolt at any cost. Besides spammers, some poor-quality SEO professionals also use bad tactics to cover their inability to do the job right.

Assuming you don't want to put your site in jeopardy, which I believe you shouldn't do, here are some questions you should ask potential vendors in order to sniff out potential spammers.

What about pricing? It's all over the map. Quality SEO firms charge thousands or tens of thousands of dollars a month. Some SEO consultants charge hundreds or thousands of dollars an hour for sharing their secrets with your team. Just remember, if the price sounds too good to be true, it's probably spam.

By the way, because SEO professionals must often sign nondisclosure agreements with their clients, you won't likely see a full client list on the vendor's Web site. Trust your intuition. If you get a funny feeling something ain't right during your conversations, run away…fast.

Questions to Ask SEO Professionals (and Answers)

Before you sign a contract with an SEO consultant or agency, do your research. Otherwise, you could accidentally hire spammers. Here are essential questions to ask potential vendors:

What performance guarantees do you make?

The answer correct answer is "none." Organic rankings are never guaranteed. Period. Organic rankings take months to achieve, and they're in a constant state of flux. Nobody can guarantee traffic either. If they say they can, they're either doing PPC instead of SEO or redirecting traffic from Web sites they've already optimized.

Will I need to change my Web site?

Absolutely. Your keywords have to be in your Web pages. Very likely, you'll also need to add more content. Anyone who says you don't need to do a thing to your site is either link spamming or redirecting traffic from optimized sites.

What's your linking strategy?

Link popularity is such an important part of SEO that this component must be addressed by whomever you interview. Ask vendors to describe their process of finding Web sites, communicating the link request, and what you'll need to do. None of this should be top-secret information. What they say should give you confidence that they're taking time to get high-quality, content-relevant Web sites to link to yours.

What kind of reports will I receive?

A significant chunk of SEO work on your Web site happens in the first few months. That's why many SEO professionals require a 6-, 12-, or even 24-month agreement. However, even though it may take months to see your site climb into top rankings, you should have routine communication with your vendor. You might receive ranking reports, as well as revenue reports. (ClickTracks, WebSideStory, and WebTrends are a few Web analytics companies whose reports can track sales from organic search.)

Spotting Snakes

I've had my own not-so-fun experiences with SEO snakes. Once upon a time, I was the vice president of online promotions for a Web agency. In the late 1990s, the agency outsourced a few clients' SEO campaigns to other firms while the agency was developing its own SEO program. We caught one of the SEO firms pagejacking, which involves stealing content from other top-ranked Web sites to get a client higher rankings. Not good. After we had fired that firm, its pagejacking tactics were later exposed by the press. Another SEO firm that wined and dined us practically disappeared once we signed the contract. We discovered later that the firm was selling an SEO service that never existed. A lack of reporting and customer service in both cases prompted the agency's investigation of, and ultimately firing of, both firms.

With those experiences under my belt, I thought I could spot SEO snakes once I became a consultant. Focused on speaking and training, I decided to recommend several SEO firms to my clients who wanted to outsource their campaign. While launching my business, a smooth-talking SEO salesman won me over with his enthusiastic talk of technology. Sigh. He burned at least two of the three companies I sent his way. Again, the lack of reporting tipped off the clients.

My own scary stories reveal the darker side of this industry. Good clients can get burned. You can protect yourself to some degree by asking the questions I've included here and being wary of firms that say they use any of the aforementioned serious spam violations as part of their strategy. Before you sign a contract, however, ask for a few references. Finally, make sure the SEO firm has a routine reporting system and follows it once you're a client. Unfortunately, sometimes it takes several months to realize you've hired a snake.

The Saints Come Marching In

Hold on. Now I've got to give praise where it's due. Many SEO professionals are saints. They're heroically battling against search engines and competitors to get your Web site to the top of the organic search results. There's no guarantee of success or of maintaining it once it's been achieved. It's an ongoing battle.

Okay, I realize that saints aren't known for their warlike ways. Maybe the "good guys" are more like knights. But "Knights and Snakes" isn't as catchy of a subchapter heading. However, if you prefer to think of the good SEO professionals as knights fighting for your Web site's visibility in the search results, go ahead. It's a fun metaphor.

While SEO saints are out to do good work, they're sometimes burned by prospects and clients. First, bad prospects request meeting after meeting to pick the brains of the good guys, never signing a proposal. Not cool. Bad prospects also demand a proposal that specifically details every tool and technique that will be used. Um, SEO professionals won't give up their hard-learned expertise. No way. And bad clients expect top ten rankings for all of their keywords within 30–60 days, without spamming, of course. That's ridiculous.

I once spent about 30 minutes evaluating a friend of a colleague's site and e-mailing her some SEO recommendations. I think this woman wanted a button that would instantly fix her lost Google rankings because she replied that her site wasn't important enough to do the kind of work I was proposing. Although I had volunteered my time, I was still irked by her response. Hopefully, by sharing my story, you'll understand the challenges search marketers face.

Let's get back to the good stuff. The topic of search engine optimization isn't complete without a "Success Story." I worked hard to collect a cross-section of companies to feature in this book. And as you might imagine, it wasn't easy convincing my clients and colleagues to share their hard-learned lessons with the public, possibly their competitors. Fortunately, my pleading paid off!

Paradise Ranch Country Clubs for Dogs demonstrates how niche businesses can rise to the top quickly with SEO. More importantly, it sheds light on an emerging trend I'll cover later in this book: the localization of search.

continues on page 22

Success Story
Paradise Ranch Country Club for Dogs

URL: www.ParadiseRanch.net

Contact: Richard Jenkins (www.WebSearchEngineer.com)

Title: Search Marketer

✦ Goals/Challenges

What were your goals for doing SEO?

Unless people knew the URL, nobody could find the Web site for relevant keywords in the organic search results. Our goal was to get Paradise Ranch to rank in the top spots for dog care services in Los Angeles (dog boarding, training, daycare, and grooming).

What challenges/concerns did you face implementing the campaign?

First, we had to redesign the Web site because it consisted of three cheesy pages that offered no relevant value to potential clients. We knew we needed quality content for the search engines, too. But before we jumped into SEO, we invested in educational resources and conferences because we were worried that we might accidentally use spamming tactics if we didn't know the search engine guidelines and rules.

✦ Strategy

Describe your implementation strategy.

We created different Web site landing pages for Paradise Ranch's main services: dog boarding, dog training, and dog grooming. We optimized each of these pages, and others, for relevant keywords. Because the dog ranch is based in Los Angeles, we focused on optimizing phrases that include "Los Angeles."

How long did it take to launch your SEO campaign?

SEO never stops! Okay, our site redesign and initial optimization of about 12 pages took about 30 days.

What problems or surprises did you encounter, and how did you resolve them?

We learned not to throw all of the keywords on the home page. That borders on spam, and adding too many keywords to one page dilutes the page so it ranks for nothing. Early on, we also made a mistake of optimizing the site for broad, highly competitive terms. Using geographically targeted keywords in SEO and PPC is a much easier and more profitable way to go. While waiting for our SEO efforts to kick in, we did geo-targeted PPC to get instant traffic.

✦ Results

What results did you achieve?

Within the first 90 days, the site landed top three positions for primary keywords in Google, MSN, and Yahoo!. Regional keyword targeting was key to our success. Paradise Ranch's business boomed. And because the cost-per-lead was so low, the ranch cut two print advertising campaigns that brought in minimal business, if any. We still do PPC because it's profitable, but we've reduced our bids or stopped bidding on expensive keywords that Paradise Ranch dominates in the organic search results.

What's your #1 recommendation for SEO marketers?

Geo-targeting is gold. There's less competition, and it's easier to achieve top organic rankings faster with regional keywords than with broad keywords.

continued from page 19

Regionally based companies can jump into search marketing without losing their shirts. And national companies can reap higher profits by tailoring their SEO and PPC campaigns to targeted communities. Jump on the local search wave, and you'll likely invest a lot less time and money for high-converting search campaigns.

Tips to Remember

Whether you're managing your SEO campaign in-house or outsourcing it, you now know the three most critical strategies you need to create a successful campaign: keyword theme, relevant content, and link popularity.

You also have a list of link and site spamming tactics to avoid. This list, and the questions for interviewing SEO professionals, should help you connect with the "white hat" optimizers, if you decide to enlist some help.

The discussion of SEO doesn't end here. Throughout this book, I'll reveal tips for optimizing your online marketing opportunities to seduce spiders while catching customers and pleasing the press. Writing articles for the Web does all this and makes you "The Expert."

2

Leveraging Articles
for the Web

Y ou don't have to be a professional writer to write articles for the Web. You do, however, need to think like an online marketer to make them bring in business.

Online articles can't be treated like offline articles. That's because online articles boast several advantages over their offline counterparts, including the following:

✦ **Web articles have "sticking power."**

They can be continually discovered by new readers and rediscovered by previous readers. What a branding benefit. And the publicity potential is high, too. Web articles can be linked to by Web sites and blogs (and passed around by e-mail). By contrast, offline articles in print-only publications don't have sticking power or viral potential. Once the offline article is no longer featured in the publication, it's out of sight.

✦ **Web articles improve your organic search engine rankings.**

When optimized for relevant keywords and linked to your Web site or blog, not only can your articles climb to the top of the organic search results, but your Web site or blog can also. Because offline articles are…well, offline, they offer no SEO value. I'm not saying offline publicity isn't great; it's just not great for SEO. Meanwhile, Web articles give you brand awareness *and* higher search engine rankings. What a deal!

✦ **Web articles drive prospects to your Web site now.**

Web articles can deliver results—fast. Offline articles can't. In order to get offline article readers to go complete an action online, you must promote an amazing offer to persuade those readers to stop what they're doing and go to a computer, if they even can. Meanwhile, with one click on a link, online readers can go from your article posted pretty much anywhere on the Web and head straight to your Web site. The road to instant gratification is short. This fact works in your favor.

Although you can write articles and publish them on your own Web site, which I recommend as one way to offer value to your visitors, that's not the focus of this chapter. Here, I'm talking about writing articles for Web sites and blogs *not* managed by you. By reaching out to readers where they are, you'll start down a path of finding fame, fortune, and maybe even fans.

Don't skip this chapter if you've already written several online articles. Although anyone can become a published writer on the Web, few understand how to leverage the Internet to its full potential. As you read this chapter, keep your mind open and allow new creative ideas to come to you.

In this chapter, I'll cover simple steps for writing Web articles that attract customers, press, and spiders to your site, while branding you as "The Expert."

Golden Opportunities

As an *Entrepreneur* magazine columnist and freelance writer, I'll let you in on a fun fact: *It's amazingly easier to write for online publications than offline ones.* Why? Well, for a few reasons.

First, there are more publications online than offline. On the Web, you can find Web sites and blogs dedicated to all kinds of topics. Even if a print publication doesn't exist for your exact area of expertise, you'll likely find several on the Web. Start your hunting at online directories like Yahoo!. When you find places you think your ideal customers visit, pitch topic ideas to the publishers of those sites (sending an e-mail is usually more effective a phone call).

Better yet, online content publishers are starving for content. They need fresh articles to attract new visitors and grow a loyal readership. One way that publishers can reduce their writing workload, while offering valuable content, is to allow industry experts to share information with their readers. This also boosts the publishers' credibility by showing they are rubbing elbows with industry players like you.

Whether you're working in-house or on your own, I'll share tips on getting visibility as an industry leader by branding *yourself* as an expert in the next section. Promoting a personal brand, even while promoting a company brand, is a very effective marketing strategy. That's because getting your personal name known opens the door to bigger opportunities for you and your company.

Attracting Clients...Fast

By writing articles for the Web, I landed my job as *Entrepreneur* magazine's "Net Sales" columnist...within 24 hours. Yup, it happened that fast. I was blown away. Actually, I'm pretty sure I was skipping all around the house when I was offered the job. Let me tell you what happened.

One of *Entrepreneur's* branding columnists who met me about a year earlier knew I did Internet marketing. The magazine was looking for an Internet marketing columnist, and the branding columnist recommended me. Within hours of getting an e-mail from the articles editor, Charlotte Jensen, asking me to send her writing samples if I was interested, I e-mailed her one of my online newsletter issues and links to free articles I had written for a marketing conference Web site. Sold! Charlotte immediately responded, and I was given the job within 24 hours.

My newsletter certainly helped. However, I bet the online articles I had written for a prestigious conference closed the deal, even if the articles editor had never heard of the conference. This gave me credibility as an industry expert. By being published on a reputable Web site, my work was essentially validated by a third party. Not only did I get exposure on the conference Web site, but also writing articles for free delivered a paid writing opportunity to my doorstep...um, I mean e-mail box.

This is just one example of how writing articles for the Web can pay off. And there's another golden tip in here, too. Did you catch it? Consider speaking at, or attending events, and writing articles for the conference Web site.

Perks of Writing for Events

Why not pitch the idea to the conference planner that you'll cover several educational sessions in exchange for a free pass or a reduced rate? Okay, that tactic usually doesn't work at big conferences. But if you're going to be there anyway, offer your freelance writing services at no charge as long as you get a link to your Web site and a byline (the author's name and possibly a short bio). You might score a two-for-one deal.

Your article could be e-mailed to the conference's online newsletter subscribers, plus it could be posted on the conference Web site for all visitors to see and spiders to find. One article, distributed through two channels.

Although being a reporter for a conference is a bonus idea to consider, it's not always as good as writing articles for other sites and blogs. That's because while covering an event, you must to stick to the sessions assigned to you. (Be sure to ask to cover sessions related to your area of expertise. That way, your byline tells prospects you can help them with the topic you're writing about.) Plus, without investing time or money attending an event, you can find plenty of writing opportunities right now simply by surfing the Web.

Wait. Writing articles for Web sites doesn't instantly make you an expert. There's a strategy to making this work. Luckily, it's not hard, although it does require a little planning. In the next section, I'll reveal a way to build your brand quickly while attracting humans and spiders.

You, the Expert

Before you start writing, stop to consider these two questions: *Where are you now* and *where do you want to be?*

By answering both of these questions, not only will you brainstorm a surprisingly long list of topic ideas, but you'll also identify the ones that will take your business where you want it to go. By establishing yourself, or your business, as "The Expert" on the issues you want to help your customers resolve, the articles you write for the Web will draw your ideal customers to you. Sounds effortless? It is.

Many business professionals aren't achieving the growth they want because they haven't defined who their ideal customers are. And they aren't sharing information to attract those customers to them. Let me give you an example.

Let's say you're a Feng Shui consultant, or you're marketing a Feng Shui consulting firm. Feng Shui is the Chinese practice of arranging a space to achieve harmony with the environment, which can create improved health, wealth, and other desired changes.

Figure 2.1 shows three possible areas of focus for a Feng Shui consultant or agency: Feng Shui for the home, office, and landscape. Many Feng Shui professionals might be tempted to write articles about general practices or overall benefits of Feng Shui. That's an excellent start.

However, the professional who wants to attract new clients interested in office Feng Shui should write about this particular topic. Readers who are looking for this information will instantly connect with this professional's highly relevant, timely articles. They'll see this professional as the expert on this topic. And they'll be motivated to hire him.

Think carefully about *"where are you now?"* and *"where do you want to be?"* because the topics you write about will be carried out to the public by search engine spiders and the press. To get this free brand-building publicity fast, be a specialist.

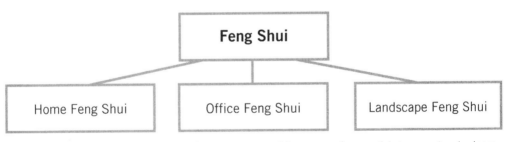

Figure 2.1   A Feng Shui consultant could focus on any one of these areas for an article to promote a business.

Be a Specialist

On the Web, the number of competitors you're up against could be overwhelming. And chances are, they're getting smarter with their Internet marketing. You don't need to spend more money than your competitors do to win free publicity as well as new business. By being a specialist, you can outmaneuver them.

Start by evaluating your chief competitors on the Web. Look up your company's most important keywords in search engines to see who your competitors online really are; they're usually not the same as they are offline. It's important to see who has top organic rankings because one of your online marketing goals is to outrank them. (Check out the Alexa Web site to get interesting data on your competitors' sites.)

Next, size up your competition. What are their strengths? What are their weaknesses? What are your advantages and disadvantages? Doing this will help you see your unique specialty. This is the message you want to convey in your Web site. And you want to develop article ideas around this specialty because your unique content will get attention online. You need to take this step, regardless of your company's size.

If you're a consultant or small business owner, specializing helps people immediately understand how you can help them. Being a generalist, on the other hand, is the kiss of death.

For example, what exactly does a business strategist do? It's a vague concept. You don't want people trying to guess how you can help them, because they won't. By contrast, a business strategist who specializes in corporate sales training, or product development is instantly understood. Specializing is a big asset online because people make decisions within seconds. Connect with them immediately or lose them. Don't worry—being a specialist doesn't restrict you from expanding your market reach. It's a way for you to get your message found more easily on the Web.

Even big brands need to scout out their smaller, and often more nimble, competitors online. Each of a corporation's product (or service) categories has an entirely different set of competitors who could be building better brand awareness and customer loyalty in those categories. Therefore, a large company can write articles to demonstrate its expertise in categories in which the company is not currently known as experts.

Even though I've been doing Internet marketing since the mid-1990s, I became known as an expert in search engine marketing, which is a specialty of Internet marketing. That's because a majority of my speaking engagements, webinars, online articles, and my first book focused on search marketing. Now as an Internet marketing columnist for *Entrepreneur* magazine, and Dean of LA College International, I often use "Internet & Search Marketing Expert" in my byline to expand my market reach. However, I won't likely ever lose the search engine focus because that's my unique specialty. What's yours?

I'm not telling you to toss your entire business model out the window. Just think about your specialty within your field of expertise. This will give you article ideas that are targeted enough to easily attract your ideal customers and information-hungry journalists. Search marketing tips and tools can help you prioritize your topic ideas. Let's look at how these work.

Seducing Humans and Spiders

Want to know an easy way to determine which topics to target first to attract human readers and search engine spiders?

Look at Figure 2.1 again. Does it remind you of something I covered in the first chapter? Remember keyword themes? You can use your site's keyword theme to create articles that will support your SEO efforts. An optimized article can get free search engine rankings. So can the Web page the article links to. Here is an example of how to use this technique.

Let's pretend a Feng Shui professional has a page in his Web site about office Feng Shui information. Here are relevant keywords I discovered by looking up "office Feng Shui" in Yahoo!'s free Keyword Selector Tool:

+ Office Feng Shui
+ Home office Feng Shui
+ Office Feng Shui guidelines
+ Office Feng Shui layout
+ Office Feng Shui colors

Each of these keywords is a great article topic. If you're looking for a Feng Shui professional to redesign your office, would you contact the author of the general article on Feng Shui or the author who wrote about office Feng Shui? The second author will probably get your business...if you find his article.

Here's how to get maximum exposure. If you optimize each article for the associated keyword(s), your online articles will appeal not only to human readers but also to search engine spiders. Your articles get a good shot at catapulting to the top of the organic search results. I'm not saying you should switch your search engine optimization efforts from your Web site to the online articles. Optimize both.

Prospects, press, and even potential partners who stumble across your online articles in the organic search results will view them, and ultimately view your business, as being validated by a third party. Having your online articles posted on reputable Web sites is similar to an endorsement. After all, site owners approved your articles because they're valuable to readers.

> ✦ *Tip: Here's a warning for all writers: Watch out for ultra-trendy topics. Because fads fade, remember to write about things that will always be timely and draw traffic. Too many professionals waste their time writing about stuff that people won't search for in the future. Think about what will interest prospects and the press several months or years from now, as well as today.*

Writing for the Web gives you instant credibility, better visibility with your ideal audience and in the organic search results, as well as a fast track to becoming a recognized expert.

Are you worried about how much time writing articles takes? Not as much as you think. There's an easy way to get your message out there, again and again, without crafting a new article from scratch every single time. No, you can't just keep submitting the same article. You've got to share more than one idea to build up your status as an expert. Plus, you'll want to avoid being penalized by the search engines for duplicate content. Quick customization helps you achieve both.

Customization Quickies

Let's say that you've identified 25 sites and blogs that would be perfect places to post an article you've written. Does that mean you have to write 25 different articles? Thankfully, no. You can save a significant amount of time by customizing one article for multiple publishers. There are several reasons why you should do this.

First, not all content publishers have the same audience. Using the Feng Shui example again, pretend a Feng Shui consultant finds two Web sites that could publish his article on using Feng Shui in the office to attract new business. One Web site focuses on home-based business owners while another focuses on corporate executives. Should the Feng Shui professional send the same article to both Web sites? No. He should change his language to appeal to each audience.

For example, home-based business owners might connect better with "grow your business," whereas corporate executives might identify more readily with "improve your return on your investment." Customizing your articles for the right audience is an easy and essential step.

Another way to customize an article is to change the example you write about. Including an example is a great way to help the audience see how your information can be applied to their individual situation. It's also a creative way to share a client's success story. Just remember to get permission from your clients to use their personal name, or company name, if you're going to share their performance results.

As a freelance writer, changing my language and using different examples lets me write about the same topic for several different publications quickly. I decide how much customization I'll do depending on the publication. Let me explain why.

When you're paid for articles, you can't repurpose as much of the content. You're being paid to write an original, previously unpublished piece of work. That almost always means you can't submit the article you've been paid for, to another publication. You're not prevented from writing about that topic again, however. Or even the core principles, steps, or tools you wrote about in the paid piece. You just can't resubmit the same article, *in its entirety*, to another publisher.

Here's what you *can* do—repurpose your steps but use a different example. Or, mention the same set of tools but apply them in a different way. Those are quick edits.

On the Web, many writing opportunities aren't reimbursed with cash. However, when you get your article posted on a Web site or blog that receives thousands of unique visitors, you can easily bring in new business that far exceeds what you would have been paid for writing that article anyway. Plus, you can leverage articles you've written for free to get better search engine rankings and valuable coverage by the media.

The problem of duplicate content is another reason why you should customize your articles. As I mentioned in Chapter 1, duplicate content generally refers to the same content posted on different URLs. So, if you submit the same article to dozens of different Web sites or blogs, that's duplicate content. And that's considered spam.

Even at recent conferences, search engine spokespeople have announced they're cracking down on duplicate content. So don't do it. You don't need to panic if more than one Web site or blog posts the same version of your article. It happens. Sometimes, content publishers take stuff they find online without asking. Unless it's a really shady spot, if they include a byline and a link to your site, you'll get more visibility without doing any work. That's not so bad.

And quite frankly, sometimes you don't have time to write original articles for each online publication, especially if it's a free promotional opportunity. Just try to limit the number of online publications that have the duplicate article. That's not great for readers or spiders to see. And do your best to customize each one quickly.

The greater your customization of each article, the less likely that it will be banned as duplicate content. That means more of your articles could rank well in the organic listings. How happy would you be if your Web site and your Web articles appeared in the top search results? Ecstatic, I imagine.

Insider Insights: Nick Usborne

Nick Usborne is an online copywriter, author, and prodigious writer of articles. Most of his articles can be found at his site for online copywriters, ExcessVoice.com.

What's the #1 mistake marketers make with writing articles for the Web?

They take the short-term view and can't resist promoting themselves in some way. This reduces their credibility from day one.

What's your favorite simple but powerful tip?

Write articles without any expectation of short-term benefits. Make your articles consistently useful and helpful, above all else. That way, you'll build yourself a deep and lasting reputation as a reliable authority on your subject...and as someone always worth reading and listening to.

How has writing online articles helped your business?

Without writing articles, I would have no business. By getting articles published on reputable sites, everything else followed. Speaking engagements, an invitation from McGraw-Hill to write a book, inquiries from prospective clients...they all came from the articles one way or another. I do nothing else to promote my services. I just write articles and wait. And so far that approach has brought me a six-figure income every year.

The Mighty Byline

An article byline includes the name of the writer and often his biographical information. It's short, yet powerful.

> ✦ **Tip:** *Check out the bylines in the "Insider Insights" sections of this book for ideas.*

Don't write articles without getting a byline. *Ever.* I mean, what's the point if you can't claim authorship of the sensational information you just shared? Your byline is a magnet for fame, fortune, and fans. Well, it can be. An effective byline contains three essential elements: Who you are, a call to action, and your URL.

For the "who you are" part, include your name, title, and company name if applicable. I say "if applicable" because if you're a consultant, then the name of your company might not be as important as squeezing in an extra title. For example, I typically call myself an "Internet & Search Marketing Expert" and either *"Entrepreneur* Columnist" or "Dean of LA College International," depending on the publication. Sometimes, I throw in "freelance writer" or "professional speaker" to attract the kind of business I want. Remember that tip from the "You, the Expert" section?

Including a call to action in your byline is essential if you can squeeze it in. Invite people to your Web site. And give them an incentive. Offer them a free e-zine, special report, consultation, tool, anything that will bring them one step closer to doing business with you...or interviewing you as a guest expert for their publication.

Write your ideal byline, but realize the publisher might edit it to fit the publication's standards. Avoiding super "salesy" speak is also a good idea. A byline that sounds too self-promotional is begging to be edited.

Finally, including your URL is mission critical—for readers and spiders to follow back to your Web site. Your business is one click away from readers who have been introduced, or reintroduced, to your business through your article. And when you dangle a fabulous free offer for clicking your URL, how can readers resist that one simple step?

When working on writing assignments, I often surf the organic search results and find a site or blog that features another company's statistics. I want those stats. So, I follow the trail by clicking the URL in the byline to get to the original source. I contact that company about being featured in my article. See how that works? If you've got great stats to share, get them out there! We journalists search the Web by following links to delicious data we know our audience will appreciate.

Search engine spiders follow links, too. An article on the Web that links to your site does two things. First, it connects spiders to your site. Second, spiders can associate the content of the article with your Web site.

Here's how. You submit an article about office Feng Shui to another site (or blog). Ask for a link from your article byline to a page within your site about office Feng Shui. Congratulations! You've increased your link popularity to your site from a very relevant Web page—your article. Remember, the sites and blogs you get links from should also feature content similar to yours. In ethical SEO, relevancy is key.

Ready for the bonus link tip? (I mentioned this in Chapter 1; however, I want to make sure you remember this.) Pay close attention.

Include your most important keyword in your byline and ask for that keyword to be hyperlinked to your site.

Forget linking your company name. That's what most people do, and it's a major mistake. Well, unless there are good keywords in your company name, or you're intentionally optimizing your company name. Link a keyword instead. Show spiders and readers why the page being linked to is relevant for that keyword.

Even if you don't get paid for your articles, having a byline and URL for the Web world to see is very valuable publicity. Of course, getting paid is always a preferred perk. Oftentimes, you can get both.

Getting Paid for Your Own Publicity

How many marketing opportunities pay *you* to promote your business? Not many. Writing articles for the Web can! Writing for free can quickly lead to writing for a fee. The best part is, instead of pitching your ideas to publishers, they come to you.

Earlier I mentioned how by writing online articles I landed my own column at *Entrepreneur* magazine. Writing a few free articles for another Web site also led to another paid writing job when that Web site owner launched a print magazine. Unfortunately, because the magazine ran out of funding, only the first issue was distributed. Still, there's another article that gives my business visibility. Plus, I can reference that article in my own promotional materials to bring in even more writing, speaking, and consulting business.

I'm sharing my own experiences to show you how quickly and easily submitting online articles can turn into paid writing opportunities. I also hope to inspire you to take action. Are you curious about what you should charge?

I need to explain something first. I'm not going to discuss copywriting services for which you're not getting a byline. You can make big bucks crafting copy for other companies' marketing materials. But because this book is about marketing your business, I need to stick to those writing opportunities. Those can include writing for traditional publications such as magazines and newspapers that have Web sites, as well as for Web-only sites and blogs. Writing for online newsletters can boost your business, but this is totally ineffectively for SEO if the newsletters aren't posted online. If spiders can't see something, it doesn't exist.

The typical range for writing articles is ten cents to three dollars per word. Many freelance writers charge one dollar per word. And some set a minimum number of words. That's a decent deal. You get to share information with readers *and* promote your business in your byline. But if you want to charge more, go for it. You might need to charge more for articles that require extensive research or interviews. Do what feels comfortable to you.

Regardless of whether you get paid or not, always evaluate the marketing opportunity.

Pete Nelson, a close colleague of mine and someone whom I've been blessed to work with, told me how writing one Web article landed him a $145,000 project. Wow! And you'll probably be stunned at how quickly the reader responded. I was. In this chapter's "Success Story," Pete shares a tactic I hope you put into practice. This technique will help you reach readers and get them to realize they need to become your client immediately.

Success Story
Everywhere Marketing

URL: www.EverywhereMarketing.com

Contact: Pete Nelson

Title: CEO

✦ Goals/Challenges

What were your goals for writing online articles?

Establish, build, and grow the relationship we have with our target audience, which are primarily women entrepreneurs.

What challenges/concerns did you face implementing the campaign?

The challenge was the same as it is for any campaign—make sure the article is relevant to the pain our audience is experiencing and provide a tangible solution that solves and/or eases that pain.

✦ Strategy

Describe your implementation strategy.

Our most successful article campaign to date was built around the topic of goal setting. Two months before I wrote the article, I issued an online survey to my newsletter list, seeking to learn what was most challenging to them and their businesses. I discovered that 86 percent of the list wanted to learn how to set better goals and plan their marketing efforts more effectively. I immediately developed a goal setting program for business owners and then wrote an article to introduce it that was titled, "In The Zone: 8 Secrets for Developing Powerful & Unstoppable Goals." At the bottom of the article was my byline, along with a one-line mention of the goal-setting program.

How long did it take to launch your online article campaign?

A little over two months.

What problems or surprises did you encounter, and how did you resolve them?

No real problems, unless you consider the number of publications that chose not to run the article. The biggest surprise, though, wasn't just how quickly we secured a major client but who the client was that really shocked me.

◆ Results

What results did you achieve?

The same afternoon that I had the goal-setting article released, I received a call from a successful CEO whom I had met three years before. Although she and I kept in touch, and she clearly knew what my company did, not once had she called me for a project to work on.

It turns out that not only did my article strike a chord with her as she felt her company's marketing and advertising goals were not being achieved, but she also told me the article gave her a new perspective on where and how I could be of value to her company.

The following week we met to discuss my company becoming the marketing agency of record for her business. Two months later we had the account. Over the course of the next 18 months, this one account generated approximately $145,000 in total revenue for our company and business partners. And it all started with an 800-word article.

What's your #1 recommendation for online writers?

When you're writing articles, don't just point out your audience's pain—educate them on their pain and provide a tangible solution. The pain you address and the solution you provide has to be relevant and real or it's not important. Of course, the solution should have some connection to the service you provide; otherwise, the reader won't be able to connect the dots from the article to your business.

Tips to Remember

Whether you do it for free or a fee, write articles for the Web.

Before you start, brainstorm topics that will bring in the kind of business you want. Then think about your specialty and evaluate your competitors to discover unique information you could share that they haven't.

To prioritize your article ideas and uncover new ideas, use keyword tools to see the topics people are looking up in the search engines. Consider crafting an article around particular keyword(s), making sure this supports your site's (or blog's) optimization strategy.

Include a byline at the end of your article that will send a stampede of prospects and press people to you, asking for more information from the expert. Finally, double-check that the URL in your byline is actually hyperlinked to your site so spiders can follow the trail, too.

Ready to super-charge your fan base? Blogs can do the trick. Blogging is big. A lot of people are doing it, but few understand how to emerge from the clutter and make their blog bring in business.

3

Blogging for Business

Everyone seems to have a blog. Your colleagues, your cousin, even your cat. Will your business die without one? No. Can a blog boost your business? Absolutely.

That is, if you create a smart blog marketing strategy. Otherwise, a blog is nothing but noise. Why? Because there are literally thousands of new blogs being created each day in the *blogosphere*, the universe of blogs. Just as with a Web site, you need to make your blog stand out from the crowd.

A *blog*, short for *weblog*, is an online journal published for the public to read. Typically, the author updates it frequently. At first glance, it looks like a Web site. Look closely, and you'll probably notice many fairly short posts organized by date. That's a blog. You can use tools such as Blogger, TypePad, Movable Type, or WordPress to create and manage your blog.

A blog gives you key communication opportunities. It gives you the ability to:

✦ Instantly publish timely information.

✦ Create a public, yet controllable, conversation with readers.

✦ Turn negative publicity into positive publicity.

✦ Build your status as an expert.

✦ Improve your organic search rankings.

✦ Get media coverage.

✦ Attract new clients.

And those are just a few of the benefits!

By comparison, a Web site seems stagnant next to a blog. Sure, you can update articles and press releases on your site. But it's not realistic to think that prospects and the press will bookmark your site to check back and see what's new with your company.

Even if you have an online newsletter, often called an *e-zine,* which is short for *electronic magazine,* only subscribers will see it. Although an e-zine is a powerful marketing tool, it's cut off from the rest of Web surfers—not to mention search engine spiders.

A blog, however, is a conversation out in the public space. Readers can stop in for a visit, sometimes post their comments, and even request direct delivery of your posts.

If you want to reach blog readers, simply spitting out company marketing materials won't work. Your blog must be personal, educational, and responsive.

Anyone Can Do It

Being responsive is becoming increasingly critical because blogs aren't solely published by companies. On the contrary. The popularity of blogging has skyrocketed because it's a quick and easy way for anyone to say anything. Everyone can be publishers. The question is: *What are bloggers saying?*

Some are saying nothing, some are saying something, and some are slamming your company. Wait. What? That's right. The blogosphere is a public relations powerhouse, which can work for you or against you.

The more visible your company is, the more likely it will be a target of good and bad press. Journalists aren't the instigators of negative news. Be on the alert for angry customers, consumer protection watchdogs, competitors, and anyone who just doesn't like you. Blogging is a highly visible outlet for unhappy people. A blog gets primetime visibility because it's juicy spider bait.

Search engine spiders scout out blogs because they are full of content that's constantly updated. Plus, blogs can attract links more easily than a Web site can. If you create a blog that serves the public, you'll continue to create a fan base that will link to your blog without you even asking them to. Because spiders love content-rich pages with quality links pointing to them, a blog can often be more appealing bait than a static Web site.

This discussion about engaging readers, responding to bad press, and baiting spiders should show that purely publishing a blog ain't marketing. Whether you already have a blog, or want to publish one, this chapter reveals sound strategies for leveraging supporters and complainers to get free publicity and new clients.

Stop Persuading, Start Engaging

First, let's start with what's on a blog. An author writes a series of posts or blog entries. Each post typically has the following features:

✦   Post title

✦   Permalink, the URL of the post

✦   Post copy

✦   Author's name

✦   Date and time of the author's post

If you let people post feedback, then you'll have a Comments section under each post. You might also show TrackBacks, which are links to other sites that mention your post.

To see a fun example of one, go to Park City Mountain Resort's Web site and click the blog link. (You'll see how the resort leverages its blog at the end of this chapter.)

Who Is the Ideal Blogger?

If you're a consultant, readers obviously want to hear from you personally.

A company's ideal blogger is the CEO, product developer, marketing manager, or someone whom readers would love to get the "inside scoop" from. You might invite several spokespeople to post. Each author could share a different peek into another side of your company. Having multiple authors also reduces the responsibility of any one person to keep the blog content fresh, which is one time management issue resolved.

Publishing your blog is not a job for an intern! Your authors are online PR spokespeople. These employees should embrace your company's values, have played on your team for a while, and understand what they shouldn't post in a public space that can reach millions of readers.

This isn't a job for your PR firm either. Blog readers want to hear from someone at your company, not your bodyguard who will publish prepared statements. Give your readers access to a real voice. And coach your blogging team to write as though they're having a casual conversation, instead of writing an article. Creating a casual conversation is an effective way to engage readers.

> ✦ **Note:** *A note to corporate executives: Your employees probably already have personal blogs, or will soon. Create a company blogging policy immediately. This generally includes a reiteration of your confidentiality contracts. And you should clearly state what should not be blogged about and communicate this information to your employees.*

What to Share

The beauty of a blog is its ability to grow your business without pushing a hard sales message at people. Yes, you should absolutely link your blog to your site, maybe even to specific products or services, if appropriate. But be careful. Overwhelming "Buy NOW!" content along with too many links to your own site will brand your blog as a big 'ole sales pitch in the eyes of your readers. You'll kill your blog.

Your job is to educate and engage. Do these two things and business will come your way. No sales pitch is needed. Leave that approach for advertising campaigns, not public relations ones.

Another blogging blunder is to regurgitate your company information on your blog. Save that for your site; it's not usually exciting stuff for a blog. To get, and keep, the attention of your readers you could share the following information:

+ Quick "how-to" tips.
+ Answers to a recent poll or survey you offered. (You could also offer a poll or a survey on your blog and ask readers to participate.)
+ An interview with an industry celebrity or star.
+ Comments about other blogs.
+ Your opinion on a recent news story.
+ Information about an event, conference, or trade show.

I'm sure you noticed that none of these are specifically about your company's products or services. You can certainly use your blog for company updates. Large corporations often use a separate blog to respond to customer service questions or announce updates to products that change constantly, like software. But assuming you're starting with one blog, think about creating content that's not always all about you.

Let's look at an example. Instead of solely talking about the products it sells, a pet supply store could write posts about:

+ Seasonal pet health tips.
+ Employees' personal stories about their pets.
+ Animal adoption events sponsored by local animal shelters.
+ A charity event the pet supply store will sponsor.
+ Ways readers can help abandoned animals after a national disaster.

You really have an unlimited number of things you can write about—although, I'm guessing that if you don't already have a blog, you're worried about investing a huge amount of time to maintain one.

There are bloggers who post every single day, and they certainly get more exposure on the Web because they're publishing more content than other bloggers. Frequency is ideal. But if you're just getting started, try blogging monthly. (If you want, you can post comments on other people's blogs for a while before you create your own. You can get some good exposure this way, too). Then increase the frequency of your posts when you're ready.

Again, having multiple authors helps share the responsibility of keeping your blog updated.

Shorter posts help also. Understand that you're not writing an article. An effective post entry can be a few short paragraphs or even a few sentences. What you say, and how often you post, is more important than your word count.

An easy way to write often, while also keeping your content engaging, is to invite readers to participate. Ask a question. Ask for success stories. And ask for ideas. Although getting feedback might seem overwhelming, that's exactly what you want.

It's a Dialogue

A blog that doesn't allow people to post comments is a monologue. Boring. It can't truly be engaging unless you create an open dialogue. A dialogue is interesting.

Some blogging tools let you prevent people from posting comments altogether, or allow you to approve comments or even moderate comments before they're posted.

Jeremy Wright, author of *Blog Marketing*, strongly suggests that blog owners allow comments to be instantly posted. Otherwise, commentators could be confused or disappointed by not immediately seeing their comments live. For publishers who stay on top of their blogs, I see Jeremy's point. But I believe you should review and then approve comments before they're posted on your blog.

That's because if you're not constantly monitoring your blog or using a tool with anti-spam features, spammers can dirty a blog quickly with meaningless comments and links used to improve their search engine rankings or their clients' rankings. Unhappy customers or crafty competitors could post terrible things before you catch them. I say, check out comments before you publish them.

This sounds scary, I know. I didn't allow comments on my blog for the first few months of its life. While I was working away on a project, I freaked out thinking about reviewing comments at 1 a.m. when I finished working. I wasn't ready. It's okay if you're not ready either. As with any of the strategies mentioned in this book, take the steps you're ready to take. Publish a blog to get the feel of posting and discover your voice.

When you're ready, be accessible. Let people post comments. You get to learn what your customers need and want. You can even get instant feedback on an existing product or service, or one you're thinking about selling—free market research. This reason alone is why you, or a blog monitor you assign to the job, should keep an eye on your blog.

Ready to blog? Not quite yet. You know how to make your blog engaging. But before you type one word, be sure that what you write will get noticed by the spiders. If you do this correctly, they'll make your content visible to a whole new world of readers.

Emerging from the Clutter

The explosion of blogs makes it a challenge for new blog publishers to emerge from the clutter, but not impossible.

Start by making the search engine spiders work for you, especially since you don't have to pay them. How much of your blog you can optimize depends on your publishing tool. First, try and fit relevant keywords in these areas to seduce spiders:

Post Title

Placing keywords in your post title benefits you in two ways. First, because the title of a post is seen by readers, it's also seen by spiders. Don't use your core keywords in every title. That's spammy.

Remember how to create a keyword theme for your site from Chapter 1? Apply this concept to your blog. Use a variety of different keywords in post titles that support your blog's overall keyword theme. This technique helps attract readers who may see your posts' titles in the search results, as well as under a "Previous Posts" or "Archives" section on your blog. (Many blog publishing tools automatically file your posts under this kind of category, not to worry.)

There's a second way a post title can attract spiders. The post title might be used in the *permalink*, the URL of that blog post. For example, if the title of a pet supply store's post for its cat blog is "5 Steps for Raising a Healthy Kitten," the permalink for that post might look something like **www.blogname.com/ 5-Steps-for-Raising-a-Healthy-Kitten**. This is yummy spider bait. Hopefully, your publishing tool creates unique permalinks for your posts. If not, it might be something you can change in your tool's settings.

Post Copy

Again, because readers see your post copy, spiders do too. So create relevant content. For example, a pet supply store's blog publisher shouldn't always post about his travel adventures without connecting his content back to pets. Irrelevant content isn't just confusing to readers, but spiders don't get it either. This pet store would have a tough time trying to rank well for pet-related keywords. The author isn't connecting his content to the company's keywords. Don't make that mistake, or it'll cost you valuable visibility in the search engines.

> ✦ *Tip: Feature your main point early in your post copy. When it's displayed in a feed reader (see the next section), people see your good stuff right away, even though they might not read the entire feed.*

Links

Blogs are great link bait, which basically means that you've got something worth linking to. Bloggers love linking to other blogs. If you've got valuable content and get the word out about your blog, you'll get links without asking. Of course, asking doesn't hurt, especially if your blog is new. Who loves links? Spiders do. As they're crawling the Web, spiders have a better chance of finding your blog if you've got a lot of links to it. And they'll reward your blog with a high link popularity score, too.

Don't forget to link to other blogs and sites. In your quest to brand your blog as an expert resource, you've got to link to others.

Blogrolling is the act of linking to other blogs. A blogroll is similar to a page of links you might have on your Web site. However, instead of creating a "Resources" page as you might for your site, a blogroll is generally placed in your blog's main navigation. You should definitely link to authority resources that are relevant for your readers. Doing this improves your status as an expert, which spiders notice as well. A blog or site with no outbound links seems awfully suspicious.

You just learned three essential steps for optimizing your blog. Simple, right? Optimizing your blog isn't radically different from optimizing your Web site. But because many business professionals don't realize this, they end up publishing a blog that's not spider friendly. Now that you know this, you can optimize yours so you can say "Come on in, spiders. This blog tastes great!"

Start with these techniques, and you'll easily attract spiders as well as the human audience. It doesn't hurt to push your content out to people. There are a lot of hungry blog readers out there—so feed them.

Set Your Blog Free with Feeds and Pings

You can't sit back hoping readers will return to your blog. A few loyal readers might. Most won't. Don't fret—they're not gone yet. You can invite them to subscribe to your *feed*. This allows you to deliver your posts to them.

There are two main types of feed standards: RSS (Really Simple Syndication) feeds and Atom feeds. Each is a format that collects and distributes content from various blogs and Web sites. You can offer one or both feeds on your blog. A feed reader or news reader is needed to display the RSS or Atom feed as readable content. Bloglines and Feedreader are examples of free feed readers.

Still with me? Offering a feed allows people to subscribe to your blog posts and receive them through their feed reader. It's kind of like a Web site visitor subscribes to your e-zine and must then check his e-mail program to read it.

I'm not going to talk about how to create an RSS or Atom feed because, well, I'm not that kind of girl. That's true geek speak; I'm only half geek. There are free resources on the Web, if you're interested in learning how to do this.

For example, FeedBurner, which is a feed management provider, offers a helpful "Feed 101" section on its site. Or you can hire an Internet geek for the implementation part. (Thankfully, feeds are built into most blogging platforms so you're not required to know how to do the technical stuff.) Let me tell you why these technologies are important and how they can be leveraged to attract sales, spiders, and status.

So far in this chapter, I've focused on attracting the attention of prospects and search engine spiders. What about the press? Getting quoted by them instantly improves your expert status and can immediately boost your business.

And if the publication is online, a link from that authority site to yours is priceless. Therefore, make your blog newsworthy.

Business professionals who understand blogging for the press are posting case studies, statistics, tips, special report summaries, and highly valuable information that is newsworthy. Please highlight this. I'm telling you what we, the press, really want. And the good news is that your prospects appreciate this information, too.

It's becoming increasingly important to offer feeds to hook journalists. Or at least post comments on blogs that do. Journalists watch blogs for story ideas and sources. In fact, many of them subscribe to blogs via news readers. If you want to increase your chances of being featured, feed the press. Because even if you've got direct access to them, sometimes your content isn't right. Other times, your timing isn't right. At some point, your news will be timely and relevant for someone's story. A feed keeps your new content in front of them.

Of course, journalists are searching the blogosphere, too. And there's another way to get their attention. Actually, you can reach spiders this way also. Ping them. It doesn't hurt them, I promise.

In the blogging world, *pinging* means telling other sites you've updated your blog. The blog publishing tool you're using might have a pinging feature. You can also use Ping-O-Matic or Pingoat, which are free services that will ping blog engines for you.

Okay, okay, you're not actually pinging the spiders of big search engines such as Google, MSN Search, and Yahoo!. However, because those spiders do crawl the results of blog engines, pinging indirectly helps you reach the major search engines. Besides, journalists as well as prospects are searching the blog engines anyway.

If you're new to blog marketing and this feels overwhelming, skip feeds and pings for now. You can come back to this section when you're ready to explore more ways to get your blog content out on the Web.

Blog marketing is taking off because it's fast and powerful. You can become famous overnight. However, there's good publicity and bad publicity. Because the blogosphere is fueled by consumer-created content, bloggers can play a significant role in your online reputation. This also means they can ignite an out-of-control fire that damages your brand without you knowing it.

Insider Insights: Jeremy Wright

Jeremy Wright (www.ensight.org) is a blogpreneur, president of blog network b5media, and author of Blog Marketing. He writes for Ensight and consults on blogging.

Photo: Jeremy Wright, CEO, b5media, Inc. (www.b5media.com)

What's the #1 mistake marketers make with blog marketing?

Blogs aren't like other marketing tools. There are different rules to play by and the audience, culture, and expectations for blog communication are completely different. The vast majority of blogs have no message and no authenticity. Engage your audience; the more you listen, the more you're listened to. And communicate in a real human voice. It's more like sitting around talking to friends at the dining room table than talking to peers at the boardroom table.

What's your favorite simple but powerful tip?

The first step to blogging is not to blog. Read blogs...for weeks. Understand what's going on, comment on articles you have an opinion on, and generally get involved in the small section of blogging that interests you. Then start a blog.

How has blog marketing helped your business?

My entire business is blog-based.

Attract Good Press, Fight Bad Press

The blogosphere is the wild West of the Web. People are posting—constantly. What bloggers are saying about your business can spread like wildfire. This can catapult your celebrity status or burn your brand. Because the rise and fall from stardom is highly visible online, reputation management is quickly becoming a critical part of Internet marketing. Pay attention to bloggers because they can support or slam your reputation.

In his book, Jeremy Wright sheds light on the frightening power of blogs. He shared that a blogger figured out how to pick a Kryptonite lock with a Bic pen and posted about his discovery. The post was picked up by Engadget, a gadget blog with over 250,000 readers a day. Then the *New York Times* and Associated

Press featured the story. Kryptonite was even hit with a class-action lawsuit. According to Jeremy, Kryptonite knew about the blog fire, but didn't respond because they were dealing with other issues of this crisis internally.

This horror story is every business professional's worst nightmare. While most companies will thankfully never experience this kind of painful publicity, it could happen.

You can stay tuned into the blogosphere with IceRocket, Feedster, Technorati, and other blog engines and directories. Search for your company name, product and service names, names of key executives, and your URL. You can also monitor these keywords through Blogpulse, which is a free monitoring tool that can be used to track blogs. It's quite handy.

To Respond, or Not to Respond

It's important to respond to unfavorable posts where appropriate. By posting your comments on blogs that say not-so-nice things about your business, you show that you're tuned in.

Your customers might be blowing up on blogs because your company didn't process their refund, answer their e-mail, or return their call. Frustrated, they're releasing their anger on their blogs. It's kinda like therapy. Try to find angry customers and let them know you care about them. Apologize, fix the situation, and tell them it's been fixed, or offer them a solution to their problem. Not only will your previously unhappy customers thank you for your response, but you'll also score major brownie points with those blog readers, who could become your future customers. Plus, the press watches blogs so your response could lead to a glowing PR opportunity. You never know.

Unfortunately, not all complainers are customers you can help. Some bloggers are simply unhappy people. For whatever reason, they decide to hurl general insults at you or your company from their blog. Other bloggers are competitors trying to smear your name. Still others are creating controversy as link bait.

Link Bait

Link bait is content created to attract links. A lot of links equals good spider bait. So, everyone should do link baiting, provided it creates valuable content with readers in mind. But be aware that a blogger might attack you or your company as a link-baiting tactic.

To my horror, while wrapping up this book, I was personally attacked on a blog for an article I had written. The post wasn't just unprofessional—it was mean and untrue. I was upset. Then something beautiful happened.

Several of my colleagues, who are also recognized experts, immediately posted comments on that blog. They attacked the personal attacks on me, defended my article's editorial integrity, praised my first book, and mentioned my long-standing reputation in the industry. And several said the personal attack was just a link-baiting tactic. Wow! I couldn't have asked for better publicity.

I also responded, explaining my side of the story without responding to the personal attacks. Next, I invited readers to debate the content of my article. The buzz was over in five days.

A few authors have shared similar stories with me; they let others jump to their defense instead of responding.

If you find yourself in a similar situation, know that you have several options. You might do nothing. You could respond. Or you may use your own blog to publicize your side of the story and invite feedback from your community of readers. On that note—whenever you're blogging, think before you post.

Legally Speaking

As reported by *The Washington Times* on October 12, 2006, a Florida jury awarded $11.3 million in damages to a woman who said she was defamed on an Internet message board. Currently, there are several lawsuits against bloggers.

Tempted as you may be to fend off a personal attack with a personal attack, or launch one, it's not a good legal or ethical idea to do so. Always be professional. What you say today might be available on the Web forever.

The bigger and more popular your blog, the better link bait and spider bait it becomes. Blogs are spider magnets. Much more so than your Web site. Although I don't suggest creating a blog solely to seduce spiders, higher organic rankings are a profitable perk. There's a dark side of blogging. Let's talk about spammers and sploggers.

Spammers and Sploggers

Wherever there are search engine optimization opportunities, there are spammers. Blog spamming is a favorite tactic because it's free, easy, and effective.

As a blog owner, you need to protect your blog from comment spammers. If you plan to hire an SEO professional, make sure you don't hire a *splogger*, someone who creates spam blogs as a way to get immediate organic rankings.

Most spammers aren't doing it for sport; they're doing it for money. Although spammers could be promoting their own company's products or services, they're more likely affiliates, ad publishers, or SEO service providers.

Affiliates promote other companies to get a commission for clicks, leads, or sales they generate. (If you have or want to launch an affiliate program, be sure to read Chapter 7, "Unleashing an Affiliate Force," first.) Spammers might also be ad publishers. For example, they could be Google AdSense or Yahoo! Publishing Network partners who get a commission when the ads on their site or blog get clicked. (Read more about that in Chapter 9, "Reaching Out Through Contextual Advertising.") Finally, there are SEO service providers who spam.

Remember in my first chapter on SEO I talked about the importance of a link strategy? Well, spammers have discovered a way to exploit it. Two popular blog spamming techniques include the following:

+ Posting comments in your blog to embed a link to the company(ies) the spammer is promoting
+ Creating splogs, or fake blogs used for spamming, to embed links to the companies the splogger is promoting

Blog Protection

Comment spamming has been around for several years. This practice was refined with guestbooks. Spammers developed a robot, or *bot*, that would search the Web for guestbooks and then post a generic comment in the guestbook, along with a link to the spammer's site. This program could post to thousands of guestbooks at a time. Compare that to running a "real" link campaign.

It takes weeks to identify relevant Web sites, ask for a link from their site to yours, possibly post a link to their site in return, and follow up to ensure your link has been posted on link partners' sites. And how many links could you get this way—a few dozen? That took too long and was too much work for spammers. They played the numbers game. They developed a bot to post to thousands of guestbooks, which tricked the spiders into rewarding them for their link quantity, not quality. It was a temporary tactic, but it worked.

Guestbook spamming tools were the predecessors to blog spamming tools. Because blog spammers buy domains to burn, they don't care about being caught. If you're allowing anyone to post a comment to your blog immediately, you could get hit by their tools at some point—unfortunately, faster and more often than you'd expect.

Again, that's why I recommend changing your publishing tool settings to give you editorial discretion over comments. If you're going to be an active blog publisher, then follow Jeremy Wright's recommendation of paying for a management tool that has an anti-spam feature that removes the obvious spam.

Keep a careful eye on your comments anyway. Comments like "Thanks for sharing such great info" or "I love your blog" should get your attention. It'll be your call to remove something that seems suspicious if you're not sure. After all, some readers might give short and sweet compliments. To investigate, check out the URL included with the comment. If it links to a casino, erectile enhancement drug, or porn site, you've been spammed.

The Rise of Splogging

Sploggers create fake blogs littered with links to sites they're promoting. A recovering spammer told me that in no time at all he can program a bot that generates thousands of content pages optimized for the keywords the spiders were crawling the Web for—in real time!

This kind of program may have aided in the splogging attack on Google's free blogging tool, Blogger, and Google's free blog hosting service, BlogSpot, in October 2005.

According to CNET News.com's article on October 20, 2005, the previous week a splogger published tens of thousands of splogs. Many of the splogs included names of well-known bloggers, which clogged the RSS readers of the people who were tracking posts by the well-known bloggers. Not to mention the fact that the blogosphere and search engines were polluted by these thousands of splogs.

continues on page 56

Success Story
Park City Mountain Resort

URL: www.ParkCityMountain.com

Contact: Krista Parry

Title: Communications Manager

✦ Goals/Challenges

What were your goals for blogging?

First, we saw it as a way to set ourselves apart from our competition and to connect with our guests and team members in a new way. Second, we wanted our blog to be and sound authentic, and certainly didn't want it to seem like another marketing ploy. So, we utilized individuals in different departments and facets of our business to blog. We felt that having a cross-section of bloggers would allow our readers to better understand the scope of our business. Third, we wanted a way to respond immediately to positive and negative items concerning the resort.

What challenges/concerns did you face implementing the campaign?

Our toughest challenge was getting upper management to approve the campaign! We had to explain how a blog could help our communication with our guests and team members. We also had to address their time-management concerns about being able to keep the content fresh but not spend all of our time doing it.

✦ Strategy

Describe your implementation strategy.

Although we didn't have a set schedule when we rolled out our blog, we did have a formal goal of having a daily post for the first few weeks after the initial blog rollout. From there we wanted to have a post at least every other day through the winter season. We did sit down with our principal bloggers to create a list of topics to post about, but we didn't set it up as an editorial calendar because we recognized that an authentic blog reflects topics that are as current as possible.

How long did it take to launch your blogging campaign?

Our initial launch took about one to two weeks. We did a soft launch; then after receiving positive feedback, we placed a link to our blog on our home page.

What problems or surprises did you encounter, and how did you resolve them?

With seven blog authors, consistency and management of who will post, when they'll post, and how often, have been our biggest challenges.

✦ Results

What results did you achieve?

In two weeks of launching our blog, we saw our blog traffic increase by 2,000 percent. We also saw it as a tool to distribute information to our guests. When one of our chairlifts experienced mechanical problems and was closed down for five days, we used our blog as a way to provide our guests with real-time information.

What's your #1 recommendation for blog marketers?

The best technique for effective blog marketing is consistent communication. Know what you want your blog to achieve and then create timely and interesting postings that'll bring people back!

continued from page 53

While I hate search engine and blog spam, I hold the tiniest speckle of admiration for SEO spammers. They're brilliant, creative people. They're outlaws of the Web. It's dangerous to hire them, and it's annoying to deal with the chaos they've created, yet I find stories of their mayhem a little fascinating. I can't help it. Okay, this extreme clogging of feed readers is not cool. That's similar to e-mail spam, which is evil.

I'm sharing information on how comment spamming and splogging work because you need to get educated on this stuff. If you're informed, you'll be able to better protect your blog from spammers, and hopefully you won't accidentally hire a splogger.

There are legitimate ways of marketing your blog. Quite frankly, for a little more work upfront than spamming, the payoffs are significantly bigger. You'll create a community of prospects, customers, and press who will see you as the expert. Spiders will notice too, and will reward your blog with extra opportunities for visibility and resulting business.

Tips to Remember

You can participate in blog marketing in two ways: post comments on other people's blogs or become a blog publisher. Both are good. Yet when you're ready, launch your own company blog.

First, think about what your readers want to hear from you as a business professional. How can you add value to their lives?

Then think about how to blog in a way that will invite the press and spiders to check you out. When they notice you, they'll carry your message far beyond your current blog readers.

To up your buzz factor, jump into social media. Even though blogs are social media, I've dedicated a separate chapter to the social communities. These are networking communities with their own sets of tools and marketing opportunities. Let's head there next.

4

Networking in
Social Media

Social media is defined as *"The online tools and platforms that people use to share opinions, insights, experiences, and perspectives with each other. Popular social mediums include blogs, message boards, podcasts, wikis, and vlogs."*

Well, this is the definition according to Wikipedia, a free online encyclopedia written by contributors with Internet access. Wikipedia is also a social site. With an estimated 67,000 active contributors working on over 4.6 million articles in more than 100 languages, it's a hot spot on the Web.

Are you wondering why all the buzz about social media?

Consumers are in the driver's seat, and they are fueling its phenominal growth. Anyone can create, share, publish, distribute, and promote his own content…or someone else's. The explosion of consumer-driven content is seen as a core contributor to a second generation of the Internet, which was coined "Web 2.0" by O'Reilly Media and MediaLive International in 2004. Today, consumers are empowered to communicate like never before. And you get to leverage those consumers to talk about your business all across the Web.

Although blogs are social media, I dedicated the previous chapter to managing your own blog because that's becoming an important part of Internet marketing. Podcasting could fit here, too; however, because podcasts can be a powerful tool for broadcasting your message to the press, I'll cover it in the next chapter. This chapter is about how to participate in social communities. These communities give users a place and a set of tools to socialize with each other. Here are a few examples:

✦   Business networking communities: Ecademy, openBC/XING, LinkedIn

✦   General social communities: Facebook, Friendster, LiveJournal, MySpace

✦   News-sharing communities: Global Voices Online, Memeorandum, Newsvine

✦   Photo-sharing communities: BubbleShare, Flickr, Fotolog

✦   Podcasting communities: iTunes, Podcast Alley

✦   Social bookmarking communities: del.icio.us, Supr.c.ilio.us

✦   Vlogging (video blogging) communities: Metacafe, YouTube

✦   Voter-based communities: Digg, Reddit

✦   Wikis (collaborative sites): eBay Wiki, Susning.nu (Swedish), Wikipedia, WikiWikiWeb

As you'll notice by looking at this list of social communities, some focus on a specific topic, such as global news. Others focus on a particular mode of communication, such as video.

A social site's speciality does matter. Not all of them are the right fit for your business. Besides, you'll want to start with very few sites anyway. Otherwise, you'll need to dedicate an entire team to social networking. You might not be ready for that.

You'll be happy to know that social media marketing is free. There's usually no cost to join or participate in a community. Creativity is the only real requirement, as well as a desire to share with others. Effective social networking gives you free exposure that can last a lifetime on the Web. And it's fun.

Your Profile Is a Marketing Tool

Many social sites let you create a member profile, which is your main Web page within the community. Don't write a skimpy profile. This is a prime opportunity to shine within that community, as well as on the Web.

Personalize Your Profile

Let's start with several ways you can personalize your profile to attract attention.

✦ **Choose a marketable URL.**

Sometimes, when you sign up for an account on a social site, you can choose the URL of your profile page. (The name of the community is usually the root domain name.)

For example, your default URL on MySpace will look something like this: "**www.MySpace.com/2567315**." Fortunately, from within your account you can choose a better URL for marketing purposes like this: "**www.MySpace. com/YourCompany**."

Choosing a marketable URL is an important step because this is often the title that will appear in the search results of both that social site and search engines. Case in point—the MySpace profile page of Nixon, a premium accessories company, currently ranks above its Web site in MSN Search for "Nixon accessories." Take advantage of a profile page for this kind of free exposure.

✦ **Customize your design.**

Usually when you sign up for an account within a social community, you'll get a standard-looking profile page. Or you'll get to choose a template design from a list of options. When you're ready, though, customize your design. This gives you a more professional image. And by mimicking the "look and feel" of your company's Web site and other marketing materials, you'll reinforce your brand.

✦ **Create content that is fun.**

Your Web site copy probably won't work for a social site—not if it's bland. To create a friendly first impression, create fun content for your profile that includes more than your mission statement. Here are a few ideas to consider:

- Talk about an issue that matters to you or your company.

- Share a short story from a company founder or executive.

- Post photos from an event that your company participated in.

- Post an employee song, photo, or video clip of the month.

Don't worry; you don't need to write a novel. A few paragraphs for your profile page are fine.

✦ **Set a friendly tone.**

Finally, use language that sets a tone. Be blunt, playful, or mellow. The words you use in your profile, and on the Web, help you connect with your ideal audience. They'll see your message and instantly think "Hey, this company (or consultant) is speaking to me!" The words you use reveal who you are and who you want to attract.

For example, Nixon's language appeals to a younger audience. The company's Web site and MySpace profile say: "We make the little shit better… Dammit brothers and sisters, you can't slap on an off-the-shelf piece and consider yourself you. Can you?"

Not the right language to sell to CEOs. But it'll certainly grab the attention of skateboarders, surfers, snowboarders, and image-conscious people who despise common accessories—Nixon's target audience.

Also, find out if you can link from your profile page. If so, link to your Web site (or blog). This helps humans and spiders follow the link trail to your business.

Leaving a Link Trail

Hopefully, you can hyperlink specific keywords within your profile to your site. This simple step can be quite effective. As you'll recall from Chapter 1, linking keywords to a site can boost the organic search rankings of the site being linked to.

Keep in mind, this technique works if your profile page is public. Social sites that require registration to see profiles are a problem for SEO. Because the profiles are "locked up," spiders can't see them. Consider this when evaluating which social sites to participate in. Don't make SEO potential the only deciding factor though, because some sites are the perfect match for your business—with or without the extra exposure from search engines.

Using relevant keywords in your profile is a powerful technique for a second reason. You'll boost your rankings in another kind of search engine—the one on the social media site. One way that users explore social sites is by typing keywords into that site's search engine. An optimized profile improves your visibility in these search results as well.

Ranking well in a community's search engine isn't your final destination. Social sites are all about making friends.

The Friend Factor

In some communities like LinkedIn, having a network of friends allows you to contact other business professionals you're connected to via your friends. In other communities like Flickr, fellow photographers can link to your photos from their list of "Favorites," link to your profile from theirs, or comment on your photos.

The more friends you have, the more people will find out about you. That's because a lot of people surf social sites by checking out the friends of their friends.

Before you go forth to make friends, surf. Although there are a number of ways to do this, and each community's features vary, start by using the social site's search engine. This helps you cut through the clutter of all of the consumer-generated content you'll see. Here are several kinds of keywords to look up:

✦ The name of your company, products, services, and key executives

✦ The names of your competitors and their products or services

✦ Keywords relevant for your business

Taking this step will show you what's already being shared on topics related to your business. You'll get the flavor of that community, too. The simple act of surfing helps you find friends. Now, you're ready to make some.

Be a Contributor

As you surf social sites, you'll notice who the chief influencers are. These people boast a high number of profile views, friend connections, comments from friends, votes, or some other designation of popularity. Influencers can introduce you to a big audience quickly.

To network with influencers, contribute to their content. The way in which you do this varies by community. For example, in response to an article, photo, audio, or video clip someone has created, you might be able to do the following:

✦ Bookmark it.

✦ Link to it.

✦ Comment about it.

✦ Rate it.

✦ Vote for it.

This is active participation in a social site. And it's a great way to make friends. By contributing to others' content, many will instantly link to your profile or content in return. This improves your visibility among community members. Plus, by contributing, you're essentially inviting members to stop by and contribute to your content.

> ✦ **Note:** *When you can comment on someone else's content, be supportive. Do not advertise. A sales pitch will cost you friends. Worse, furious community members could retaliate by using social sites to instantly spread hateful sentiments about you or your company. Plus, your self-promotional comment could get deleted and future comments from you could be blocked. So instead, share helpful information. Give advice or share a story. Most importantly, offer praise where it's deserved.*

Don't limit yourself to making one-on-one connections. Jump-start your network by inviting the Web world to check out your profile, or content, and be your friend.

Get Connected

By commenting on the published work of others, those people may check out your content and comment on it. If you can contact them directly about giving you feedback, and possibly a link, do so. This is why saying something nice about their work first is an asset. By being supportive of them, you encourage them to be supportive of you.

Be sure to tap into your existing community of fans who aren't yet aware of your presence on social sites.

For example, you could link to your profile page (or newly published piece of content) from your site, blog, e-mail announcement, press release, online ad, or any other marketing campaign.

Nixon links "Nixon MySpace" from its Web site to its MySpace profile for two reasons: First, to tap into its existing site traffic. Second, to boost its organic search rankings for its MySpace profile. Nixon believes that in the future its fans might look up "Nixon MySpace" in the search engines. That's possible.

Journalists who are looking for success stories about social media marketing might run this kind of keyword search as well. You never know. That's why it's important to optimize your social media campaigns for social site members and search engine users. The press will find you in either case.

Not all social sites offer a member profile page. And even those that do might give you the chance to optimize your content such as articles, photos, audios, or video clips. This is where tagging is beneficial.

Tagging, the Social Bookmark

Tags are keywords assigned to a piece of content. Tagging is a part of the social bookmarking practice in which content producers and social site users can classify, organize, and search content by keywords. Sites such as Del.icio.us, Flickr, Technorati, and YouTube support tagging.

Tagging is important because it gives your content greater exposure within social sites as well as in search engines. In this section, I'll cover how to improve your visibility in both.

Social Site Visibility

Tags help your content get found within a social site. To see how this works, it's best to see tags in action. Go to Flickr, a photo-sharing site, and type in a keyword. Up comes a list of relevant photos. Next to each photo, you'll see a tag icon with keywords next to it. Thanks to these tags (and the photo title), Flickr knows which photos are relevant to a user's keyword search.

Notice how the tags are hyperlinked? Click one. It takes you to another set of photos that are tagged with that same keyword. Flickr does this automatically. All you need are tags. Although members may create them for you, start your content on the right track by creating an initial set. This encourages members to tag your content, too.

You want social site users to tag your content as well. This helps you see which keywords people use to identify you and your business. Talk about an insightful market research feature! Plus, it's free.

Tagging also lets you leverage other members' content. That's because if their content is popular, and you use the same tags they do, people can get to your content by clicking a tag that links to it. While you're getting familiar with a social community (as I talked about in the last section), check out the tags being used for content similar to what you'll publish and consider using these keywords in your tags.

Are you curious about what are the top keyword searches in a social site? Just click the "Popular Tags" kind of link on the home page. You may see a *tag cloud,* a list of popular keywords arranged in alphabetical order; the most popular ones are displayed in a bigger font or set apart by a different visual treatment. Periodically monitoring this list can give you new keyword ideas to use in your tags. It's similar to using keyword tools that show you the popular searches on search engines. Speaking of search engines...

Search Engine Visibility

Tagging should be part of your search engine optimization strategy. Because tagging is all about linking and developing relationships, you should use some of the same tactics you use for improving your Web site's link popularity.

Use your Web site keyword list to guide you in selecting tags. Remember to choose keywords that relate to your content, as well as your business. Tags aren't just useful to search engine spiders, but can drive significant traffic to your site.

Think of your tags as links. By using tags, you are providing the keywords you want associated with your business. Plus, because you can link your pieces of content to your profile page (which has a link to your Web site) or directly to your Web site, you're ultimately boosting the link popularity of your Web site by tagging your content. Each link is yet another link vote for your site.

> ✦ *Tip: Be consistent with how you tag your content. Doing this gives you more entries with the same tag—hence more search power. You're creating your own tag cloud around your content.*

While we're talking traffic here, don't forget that you can republish your work from your Web site or blog using an RSS or Atom feed. (See Chapter 3 for information on feeds.) If you do this, people will probably subscribe to your feed to receive your content through their feed reader, or even republish your content on their own Web sites and blogs. The more content you have published on the Web, the better. Spiders will notice all of that relevant content and all of those links pointing to your business.

When you think about driving traffic with social media, there are two keys.

First, because social media is all about linking, it has a natural fit into your link-building efforts. Therefore, be sure to include social media in the mix.

The second key is that spiders use tags like users do—to determine what the article, picture, or page is about. Having a lot of social site users applying the same tag to your content enhances its link reputation for the keyword in the tag. To get high rankings in the organic search listings you must be relevant for a keyword, and having many relevant tags accomplishes this.

Insider Insights: Amanda Watlington, Ph.D., A.P.R.

Amanda Watlington, Ph.D, APR (www.SearchingForProfit.com), is a search and social media marketing expert, speaker, and consultant who has been working with the Web since 1993.

What's the #1 mistake marketers make with social media?

Attempts to go "commercial" before trust is earned, and value is delivered, can result in a serious backlash. Pretenders are frowned on, and when "outed" can find themselves portrayed as liars, parasites, or worse. Content offered freely in social media networks should be of genuine value to others in the community.

What's your favorite simple but powerful tip?

Get to know the community. Comment on what others have said. Enter the conversation with appreciative inquiry. Post an authentic profile that reveals who you are and why you consider yourself "one of us." Once established, you can legitimately explore the potential market value of the community.

How has social media helped your business?

As someone who is often quoted in social media, corporate marketers come to me wanting to know how to create an authentic and effective presence in this space.

Going Viral with Video

There are videos on the Web that are watched by millions of viewers. That's because a powerful video generates instantaneous buzz by being linked to, talked about, and passed along to others. And video producers don't pay a dime in advertising fees. Want to be one of them?

All you need is a video recording device such as a camcorder, Web cam, digital camera, or even a cell phone with a video recording feature. Next, you'll need to create a Web-ready file; .mov (QuickTime), .avi (Windows), and .mpg (Moving Picture Experts Group) are a few common formats. These days, video recording devices might automatically save the files in one of these formats for you. (You may want video editing software like Apple iMovie or Windows MovieMaker to enhance your clips.)

Online video marketing is one of the most fun and creative campaigns you can launch on the Web, and it's got huge viral potential. By leveraging video-sharing communities, you can reach millions of consumers who are ready to view, rate, discuss, and pass along your visual message to others. Are you up for the challenge? Even though video marketing isn't right for everyone, it can be a very powerful campaign for those who can do it well.

Before cameras start rolling, determine the call to action you want people to take once they watch your video. (If this campaign is strictly for branding, then you might not need viewers to do anything—yet. That's okay.) Unless you offer ads on your Web site and just need eyeballs, "getting traffic" is not your answer. It's the step after that. For instance, by promoting your URL in your video, the primary action you want viewers to take could be to:

+ Buy a product or service.
+ Enter a contest or sweepstakes.
+ Download information.
+ Request information.
+ Forward information to a friend.
+ Give feedback or take a survey.
+ Join an e-mail list.
+ Make a donation.

By determining your call to action, creative visions will pop into your head. Brainstorm ideas with your team. Nothing is too wacky, as long as you tie the video back to your business. In fact, the wackier, the better.

Infotainment Prevails

"Infotainment" is paramount. Think light on information, heavy on entertainment. These videos scream for attention. In case you're struggling to come up with video ideas, here are a few that will hopefully ignite your creativity:

✦ A how-to demonstration

✦ An interview or action clip of a company founder, executive, or spokesperson

✦ A "what not to do" enactment (either using your product/service, or which might require the need for your product/service)

Your videos don't need to be sidesplitting hilarious, although that can generate enormous buzz. By entertaining, I mean engaging.

Have you seen the "Dove Evolution" video yet? I first saw it on YouTube. It mesmerized me along with over a million other viewers. In less than a minute, a woman is transformed with make-up, lighting, and computer enhancements to create a supermodel image.

It's not funny, but it is engaging. And surprisingly, it doesn't pitch Dove's beauty products. The call to action in the video is "Take part in the Dove Real Beauty Workshop for Girls," and it shows a URL where viewers can find workshop and self-esteem building information.

Unfortunately, I couldn't get clearance from Unilever's legal department to share Dove's amazing performance statistics before this chapter was due. However, search for "Dove Evolution" in your favorite search engine to see the impressive media coverage this video has received in less than 30 days of being released, as well as the buzz it continues to generate.

> ✦ *Note: By producing a wildly popular video, you can also score an additional shot of star status within video-sharing communities. That's if your video catapults onto that community's most viewed, most highly rated, or most discussed list. Typically, these lists are featured on the community's home page and as main navigational options. Holding a position on this list for a day, week, month, or longer will earn you extra exposure because a lot of people check out these "Most Popular" kinds of lists.*

Compelling content isn't all you need to generate buzz about your videos. Get spiders to help.

Optimizing Your Videos

To reach millions of potential viewers immediately, upload your videos to communities such as BlipTV, Metacafe, YouTube, AOL Video, Google Video, Yahoo! Video, and others. Look for an "Upload Your Video" kind of link on the home page for instructions. And be sure to use relevant keyword tags and submit your files to relevant topic categories, where possible.

You might also want to drive viewers to your Web site directly to watch your videos. In that case, you can host them on your site. (You'll need to carry multiple video formats so most everyone can watch them.) Optimizing videos is similar to optimizing podcasts, which I'll cover in the next chapter. Here are a few things you can do:

✦ Use keyword-rich file names for your video files. These file names are more memorable and add a small bit of relevancy for spiders.

✦ Use keywords in your video titles and descriptions for RSS feeds.

✦ Put your videos on *landing pages* (Web pages people "land on"), and optimize those pages for relevant keywords. (The page will draw the video from another source.)

✦ Build a video sitemap, a Web page that lists all of your videos and links to them. Most people view multiple videos in a single sitting, so make sure that they can get to all of your videos from one place.

✦ Offer a keyword-rich, text-based summary of each video on your landing pages and video sitemap. By having both landing pages and a sitemap, you get two chances to be found by spiders and humans.

✦ Use relevant keywords in the links to your videos.

No discussion of social media is complete without talking about *mashups*, new content that is created from multiple sources. This is something you may want to get involved in. It's something you also need to watch out for.

Marketing Through Mashups

To understand the concept of a mashup, think of a musical mashup, which refers to songs that are made up from parts of other songs. That process creates something new. Well, Web users are taking articles, audio clips, video clips, and any other content they can get their hands on, to create new content, too.

Sometimes, people use an application programming interface (API) to publish online content from multiple sources on their own Web sites. Perhaps they use an RSS feed for this. This kind of Web site is a mashup. People also create a mashup by adding a Google or Yahoo! map to their sites, which is useful in guiding people to their places of business. Using tools to add third-party content to your Web site (or blog) can enhance your visitors' experience.

Often, users focus on mashing up one particular piece of content—a video clip, for example. On YouTube, there are already dozens of mashup parodies of Dove's Evolution video. Innovative users have lifted Dove's music, stage backdrop, or specific words to produce the evolution of a pumpkin, slob, zombie, and other interesting characters. These have been viewed tens of thousands of times. Mashups are part of the social media culture.

However, the mashing up of someone else's content can cause legal trouble for the masher if the owner of the original content decides to file a copyright infringement lawsuit.

A parody that mocks a person or company is even more troublesome. Just because parodies are shown on television and the Web, doesn't mean the producer of one is legally protected. Because being funny in social sites can be an instant buzz-builder, let's look at possible problems with parodies (and mashups) so you can better protect your business.

Getting Sued for Being Funny

Cliff Ennico, a small business legal expert and author of *Small Business Survival Guide*, sees lots of potential trouble with parodies.

According to Cliff, there really is no way you can be 100 percent protected when you do a parody of someone else's content. If your parody is truly offensive and makes the subject a laughingstock, he is going to hire a lawyer and come after you.

In the United States, the "freedom of speech" clause of the First Amendment to the U.S. Constitution protects parodies to a certain extent. But if someone sues you, you'll need to spend time and money convincing a court that the First Amendment protection applies to what you did. Cliff shares five ways someone can try to legally shut down your parody or mashup:

1. **Defamation of Character (or libel and slander)**

    Your published work contains false or misleading statements of fact about the subject (a person or company).

2. **Copyright Infringement**

   You are using the subject's copyrighted material without his permission, or in violation of his published "copyrights and permissions policy."

3. **Misuse of Trade Dress (or trade dress infringement)**

   Your published work copies the subject's product design, packaging, or image so closely that people could actually believe your work came from the subject.

4. **Unfair Competition**

   If your published work targets a competitor, he may claim it is "unlawful, unfair or fraudulent." You really don't know if something is "unfair competition" until a judge or jury makes the determination.

5. **False Light Invasion of Privacy**

   You publish information about a subject's character, history, activities, or beliefs that places him before the public in a false light.

Generally speaking, Cliff says that the creation of false or embarrassing information that ends up damaging someone's (or a company's) reputation can pave the way for a lawsuit. If you have a question about your mashup or parody idea, get thee to an attorney.

Play It Safe

If you're interested in making sure you don't accidentally infringe on someone else's copyrighted work, as well as protect yours, you may find the book *Fair Use, Free Use and Use by Permission: How to Handle Copyrights in All Media* (by Lee Wilson) helpful. Also check out the Chilling Effects Clearinghouse Web site, which helps Web users understand the protections the U.S. First Amendment and intellectual property laws give to online activities.

Of course, if you use your own content for your own mashups, you're at least safe from a copyright infringement suit.

You could also invite Web users to create a mashup using your content. This idea comes from Dr. Amanda Watlington, a social media marketing expert and contributing author of this chapter. She suggests that if you want to really experiment, promote a mashup contest like a handful of large brands are already doing on sites such as YouTube. Invite innovative consumers to show off their talents. What a fabulously fun way to engage participants and observers. What an enormous branding opportunity for your business, too.

Consider launching a PR campaign to alert the press about your mashup contest and get them involved.

> ✦ **Note:** *Your Web site should contain a "copyrights and permissions policy" explaining when you will (and won't) agree to allow others to use your content without permission. An attorney can prepare one of these for you for about $200 to $300.*

Although I've focused on you being the producer of mashups and parodies, you can certainly apply the information in this section to your business if your content is being used by someone else. Legal action is an option, especially if your competitors are the producers of such content.

However, if consumers are doing the producing, think carefully before responding with a nasty response or legal action. These publishers could be your loyal fans showing off their artistic skills. Even a less-than-favorable mashup or parody is still free publicity for your business. Sometimes, your angry response can draw even more attention to it anyway. I'm not saying to ignore content that you feel is damaging your brand or violating your legal rights. But because your response may be highly visible on the Web, it's a very good idea to involve your public relations and legal teams before responding to consumers.

Success Story
Nixon

URL: http://www.nixonnow.com

Contact: Andy Creighton

Title: Online Sales/Marketing Manager

✦ Goals/Challenges

What were your goals for your social media campaign?

Nixon's overall age demographic is broad. But online, it's a younger audience. They don't like e-mail. They like MySpace. We view each "friend" like an e-newsletter subscriber—someone who has expressed an interest in a connection to our brand. Our goals were to build a new database of interested users, show a more personable side of Nixon, introduce Nixon to friends of our friends, and drive traffic to our site cost-effectively.

What challenges/concerns did you face implementing the campaign?

We wanted the right mix of product and personality. We also had some brand concerns, as MySpace has its share of "haters" in our target market. So we didn't and won't advertise the campaign. We had to grow it virally.

✦ Strategy

Describe your implementation strategy.

We had to do it up the Nixon way; it had to be cool and different. So we created our ideal page design in Photoshop. Next, a designer used Cascading Style Sheets to cover up the generic MySpace layout and embedded the various Flash components into the design. To promote our MySpace page, I started by adding a few "friends" to our network, who in turn added us to their friends list. For SEO, I then linked the text "Nixon MySpace" from our Web site to our MySpace page.

How long did it take to launch the campaign?

Not including internal discussion on the design look, it took our team about 45–50 hours.

What problems or surprises did you encounter, and how did you resolve them?

Soon after our launch, MySpace rolled out some code that disabled linking out of Flash. Because about four of the seven Flash components linked to our site for more information, our traffic potential was immediately hindered. We're working on fixing this now.

✦ Results

What results did you achieve?

We couldn't drive as much initial traffic because of the Flash problem. But, one big result of all of this was the explosion of our friend network. Think of each friend as an e-mail subscriber. At our current growth rate, we'll surpass the number of e-mail addresses in our database in one year from now. It has taken Nixon seven years to build our current e-mail database. To me, that's amazing potential. We've exponentially expanded our reach on the Web. And most importantly, with a low, one-time cost of hiring a freelance designer along with using our in-house designers, this campaign paid for itself many times over soon after launch.

What's your #1 recommendation for social media marketers?

It won't work for every brand. Make sure that your market is there, and that it's a good fit. Ask yourself, "would people put a sticker of my company's logo on their cars?" Sure, a student loan company probably salivates at MySpace's audience, but how many college students really go around giving props to their loan company? Don't exploit this medium because keep in mind, it's easy to delete a "friend.'"

Tips to Remember

Social sites are powerful communities for building your business. Before you publish content, do your research. Surf communities to see which are good fits for you, who is saying what about topics related to your business, and who the key influencers are. Think before publishing content and consult with a PR person or lawyer, if necessary.

When you're ready to dive in, personalize your profile page and share content in that community—articles, audios, or video, for example. Be sure to optimize your content with tags and links for better visibility within that social site, as well as for search engines. To increase your exposure, make friends. Do this by contributing to the content that others have created—comment on it, vote for it, or somehow show your support for stuff you think deserves it.

By leveraging consumers, your business can benefit from massive exposure on the Web. This attracts journalists. But you certainly don't need to wait for them to find you. If you're ready for the press to share your message with the world, you can broadcast it directly to them.

5

Broadcasting Your
Message

Getting quoted by the press offline is great. Getting quoted by the press online is even better. That's because the benefits of online media coverage are the same as they are for online articles. Online publicity from the press:

✦ Has sticking power.

✦ Improves your organic search engine rankings.

✦ Drives prospects to your Web site now.

However, there's a big difference. Writing Web articles gives you immediate exposure, and it improves your expert status. But getting quoted in a major news outlet gives you instant authority. You've been interviewed because you *are* the expert—or so the public assumes.

I'm not suggesting that you skip writing Web articles to hunt down journalists instead. Oftentimes, your articles guide journalists to you. They'll follow the URL in your article's byline to your site.

Unfortunately, journalists might not find your Web articles. That's why you want to broadcast your message to them.

In this chapter, I'll talk about low-cost ways to reach the press online. I'll discuss the ways you can use to connect with three audiences at once: press, prospects, and spiders. That's optimized marketing—because even when targeting the press, you don't want to ignore the other two audiences.

Speaking of spiders, the publicity you achieve from news sites and blogs can carry significantly more weight than publicity from other kinds of sites and blogs. That's because news sites exude expert status. They publish a lot of content and have huge link popularity. News sites are authority sites. So, a link from an authority site contributes to your site's authority status. Spiders notice this. And it gets better.

Other Web sites and blogs often publish articles from news sites. That means the publicity you scored once might be rebroadcast across the Web in dozens, even hundreds, of locations. Not only do more press people and prospects see you've been quoted, but spiders find even more links pointing back to your Web site. It's a double publicity punch.

Before I tell you how to take your message to the media, I'll cover what makes a story newsworthy. Journalists are constantly bombarded by business professionals trying to get media coverage for themselves or their clients. Many miss the mark. And they miss their opportunity. Although I can't speak for all journalists, I'm going to reveal strategies that I know work…because they've worked on me. You might be surprised to learn how easy it is to attract attention.

The Newsworthy Story

A lot of business professionals make the same serious mistake when communicating with the press: *They pitch themselves, not a story.*

Even though journalists are paid by content publishers, the clients are considered the content readers, listeners, or viewers. Journalists are responsible for sharing information that serves their audience. You won't find every story to be of value. Some aren't. Just join me on this path for a moment, and you'll see my point.

Two Critical Questions

Your story is not newsworthy unless it answers two questions: *Who cares?* and *Why now?*

For example, your business, product, or service by itself is *not* newsworthy—even if it's new. Correction—it might be of interest to a journalist who specifically reviews new products and services. But for most journalists, there's no story. Not yet.

What information can you share that will benefit your audience? Value can be found in three kinds of information: statistics, case studies, and how-to tips.

Sharing Stats

There's always a demand for statistics because numbers reveal trends and trend changes. Statistics can often set the angle for a story—that is, if the stats suggest the audience needs to do something.

For example, an e-mail marketing agency could release a study that reveals 24.8 percent of opt-in e-mail is blocked by spam filters, up 5 percent from six months ago. Whoa. This statistic could persuade business professionals who rely on e-mail marketing to take action. Therefore, it's interesting to journalists. The agency should include the timeframe of the study, number of e-mail messages evaluated, and other background information. Including information on how the agency collected the statistics shows journalists the scope of the study, and it helps them determine if it's a good match for their audience.

> ✦ *Tip:* *I'm always on the lookout for new sources of statistics because generally the magazines I write for can't often quote the same company; it might seem as though the magazine is playing favorites. I like including stats because they show why the topic I'm writing about is important to my readers.*

Catching Interest with a Case Study

A case study is great journalist bait, too. Journalists often like to share real-world examples their audience can relate to. As with statistics, a case study supports the topic they're covering. Sometimes, a case study becomes their story. I recommend following a *challenge–solution–results* model. Explain the challenge your company (or client) faced, the action steps taken, and the results.

Here's where people who want press coverage mess up. They give generic information. Saying something like "we wanted more sales, so we launched a pay-per-click campaign and doubled our business" isn't newsworthy. I get this kind of e-mail all the time. Be specific. And say something unique.

For example, an e-mail marketing agency could share that its challenge was to reduce its pay-per-click budget by 10 percent, while maintaining its existing lead flow (good—that's specific). Then the agency could state how over 30 days, it tested three different ads in an effort to pre-qualify prospects before they clicked the ad. If the agency included the three ads in the case study, that would be most delicious.

For instance, the first ad mentioned the agency's minimum contract cost, the second ad mentioned a few of the agency's Fortune 500 clients, and the third ad mentioned the agency's minimum contract length. Each ad sent prospects to a different landing page showing a unique phone number. (The solution could be beefed up, but you get the point.) Although the agency expected the Fortune 500 ad to increase the agency's spend on pay-per-click, with far fewer clicks than the other two ads, it actually reduced the agency's monthly budget by 15.5 percent yet increased the agency's lead flow by 32 percent. (The agency could continue to explain what the surprising results might suggest.)

See how juicy this case study is? My mind is racing with story ideas. An obvious angle is how to reduce costs in the increasingly costly space of pay-per-click, a very timely topic. However, the importance of ad testing is interesting also. Tracking phone leads and sales from the Web is yet a third idea. If you pitch a case study to the press, include the details—those sell story ideas.

Are you wondering why an e-mail agency would pitch its pay-per-click success, not e-mail success, as a case study? Pitching the press on how you used your own products or services to achieve success seems too self-promotional. You're basically giving yourself a testimonial. Not newsworthy.

Instead, when using your company as a case study, share a strategy that's not part of your core business. If quoted, your company name and a brief description of your company are generally included in the story anyway. You could also use one of your clients as a case study. Remember to get their permission first.

Giving How-to Tips

Third, how-to tips grab journalists' attention. Again, be specific and unique. I highly recommend surfing the Web for articles that have been written on your topic idea. Don't repeat what's already been covered in the media. Figure out your unique angle. A bulleted list of tips works fine.

Using my e-mail marketing agency example once again, this agency could create a "7 Steps for Improving Your E-Mail Delivery by 50 Percent" tips list. Would this title grab your attention? It would catch mine.

And in an effort to save time, journalists might not interview you, but might include your tips. Perfect. That's less work for you, too. And you won't miss your moment of glory. Remember, journalists are always on a deadline.

On occasion, business professionals I've tried to interview missed being quoted because they didn't return my call or e-mail within 24 to 48 hours. On the flip side, as an entrepreneur, I've occasionally missed being quoted because I couldn't connect with a journalist within that timeframe. A tips list can save the day. You can send it to journalists who have contacted you, in case you get caught in a game of communication tag. A missed interview doesn't have to mean a missed publicity opportunity.

Now that you've got the inside scoop on what press people want, are you ready to broadcast your message to them? Because this is an Internet marketing book, I'll focus on three key online channels for reaching the press, which can also be leveraged to attract prospects and spiders: press releases, Internet radio/podcasts, and webinars.

Press Releases with Power

I know you might be thinking, *"Press releases are dead."*

No, they're not. Actually, press releases have been reborn. Thanks to the Web, they not only give your company a high degree of visibility with journalists, but also with prospects, potential partners, investors, and anyone else surfing the Web. And, of course, search engine spiders.

Today's news distribution service providers don't just send press releases to the media via fax and e-mail, which could easily wind up in the trash can or folder. Companies such as ArriveNet, Business Wire, PR Leap, PR Newswire, and PRWeb may distribute your press release to Web sites and even news search engines such as Google News, MSN News, and Yahoo! News. (Click on "News" from the search engine's home page to see where this information is located.) News sites and search engines might archive your press releases for up to 30 days. It's a much better deal than the one-time fax or e-mail, isn't it?

Press release optimization is a hot topic.

With so many people searching news engines, you should include press releases in your SEO strategy. Otherwise, you'll miss getting a higher level of visibility in the news engines when people, both the press and the public, search for a keyword that's relevant to your business.

And the traditional search engine spiders are scanning the news engines as well. That means you can get double search visibility—in news engines and search engines.

Besides optimizing your press release title and copy for relevant keywords, make sure that you link to your Web site (or blog). Is this sounding familiar? It should. It's the SEO strategy essentials I discussed in Chapter 1: *keyword theme*, *relevant content*, and *link popularity*.

Choosing a Distribution Company

Before you choose a press release distribution company, find out if the reports provided include search engine information. This should be free. You'll see which search engines and keywords were used to find your press release, and that is critical for SEO. And it's helpful for figuring out where your human audience is coming from and what they're interested in.

These reports tell you what people are doing with your press releases, too.

When I launched a press release campaign through PRWeb to promote my first book, I was initially disappointed. For the first few days, even weeks, the only direct response I got came from other newswire companies pitching their own services.

Fortunately, I happily discovered that my press releases were being viewed, printed, and even rebroadcast by looking at PRWeb's statistics reports. Whew. I *was* getting visibility!

Remember to look at your statistics reports to gauge the online visibility of your press releases and your business. Then surf the news engines and search engines. Just because journalists aren't contacting you doesn't mean you're not getting publicity online.

Following the PR Trail

By looking up my book title in the search engines, I spotted sites and blogs that published my press releases as articles. Fabulous. They didn't change a word. This will undoubtedly happen to you. Be ready. Carefully write press releases knowing they'll be rebroadcast for you all over the Web…for free.

As it turns out, I did get interviewed by three publications within a few months of launching my press release campaign. That was an appreciated bonus.

Press release optimization isn't just for search engines. You can optimize the content to connect better with the press and the public. Several news distribution services now allow you to include photos, audio, and video with your press releases. Talk about getting attention!

Not all companies need to test these technologies. But being an early adopter can help your human audience cut through the clutter of information online and zoom in on your message. That's something to consider.

There's one more level of optimization to think about. So far, I've talked about how to position your press releases to reach people who are searching the Web. However, wouldn't it be better if they signed up to receive this information directly from you? Of course.

The Value of a Feed

Even though the newswire services might fax or e-mail your press release to media representatives, journalists are increasingly subscribing to RSS (or Atom) feeds. Some newswire service providers automatically convert your press releases into an RSS feed, or allow you to do so easily.

As I explained in Chapter 3, RSS (or Atom) is a format that allows content to be collected from the Web and syndicated to anyone who subscribes to the feed. Subscribers use a feed reader to receive and view the content you distribute via a feed. A feed reader is significantly more spam proof than e-mail programs, which is driving the popularity of this tool.

The growing frenzy over feeds is happening with the press and the public. So once again, by distributing your press releases via RSS (or Atom) feeds, you'll be reaching three audiences at once: the press, the public, and spiders. Feeds are good spider bait and can appear in the organic search results and blog engine results.

Have you changed your mind about press releases being an outdated marketing tactic? I hope so. The news distribution services are making it pretty painless to go high-tech without being a techie.

There's another non-techie way to broadcast your message on the Web, and it's fun. You can leverage the power of Internet radio and podcasts.

Famous on Internet Radio and Podcasts

Internet radio is broadcasting over the Internet to your computer. To hear live shows you typically need Windows Media Player or RealNetworks RealPlayer. The easiest way to find out if you already have either one installed on your computer is to go to an Internet radio station, such as wsRadio.com, and click on a live or archived show.

These days, Internet radio stations offer their shows as podcasts so listeners can tune in while they're on the move by downloading the files to their iPod or other portable audio player. The stations might also offer a transcript of the show, or at least a heading and summary, via an RSS feed. Internet radio may even be broadcast to your cell phone.

Want fame without a lot of work? Be an Internet radio guest. You'll immediately tap into the station's listening fan base. The stations will likely turn the shows you're on into podcasts, saving you from having to do that work yourself.

Internet radio stations are popping up all over the Web. Some are the traditional radio stations going online, and others are Internet-only. You're not looking for the music programs, you're looking for Internet radio talk shows—guest experts are always needed.

Often, there's a "Be a Guest" link on the home page. If not, you can surf the program guide and then e-mail your topic ideas to the appropriate program hosts. The three types of information I mentioned in the first section—statistics, case studies, and tips—could be turned into timely and tasty topics.

Hosting your own program is also a possibility. Just be careful. You'll be committing to hosting, managing, and possibly promoting your show. While the

Internet radio station might promote your show in its program guide, you could be required to sell ads or pay a fee until your show is self-supporting. Yikes.

I'm not saying hosting your own show is a bad idea. It could be great. After all, you'll get online visibility and improved credibility. You could create new business opportunities by interviewing people on your show. Plus, you'll become a member of the press, which definitely has its perks.

Just think carefully before committing to being a host. Find out the station's audience reach, as well as your required responsibilities and marketing opportunities, before signing up.

Whether you host an Internet radio show or appear as a guest, your message will be available for all to listen to long after the show airs. As I mentioned earlier, Internet radio stations are archiving shows on their sites as Windows Media Player or RealNetworks RealPlayer audio files, transcripts offered via feeds, or podcasts.

Many people are essentially running their own Internet radio show by publishing podcasts. If this is you, here are a few quick tips for optimizing podcasts for the search engines:

✦ Use keywords in your podcast titles and descriptions for RSS or Atom feeds.

✦ Consider putting podcasts on landing pages (see Chapter 8) and optimize those pages for relevant keywords.

✦ Offer a text-based summary or transcripts of each podcast on your landing pages.

✦ Submit your podcasts to sites and directories such as iTunes, Odeo, Podcast Alley, podOmatic, Podscope, and others. Submit your podcasts to relevant categories within directories, where possible.

✦ Use relevant keywords in the links to your podcasts.

You don't have to jump on the podcasting bandwagon. Instead, contact Internet radio shows and highly visible podcasters about being interviewed. Leverage their techie skills. All you have to do is talk.

I recently searched for my name on Google's Blog Search and spotted several podcasts of interviews I did. Cool. Internet radio shows, and podcasters, will promote you for you. This can lead to additional media coverage and new business. One of the podcasts I did resulted in a paid speaking job within 30 days of being posted. The same can happen for you.

The fun part about Internet radio is being able to call in from anywhere to do the show. All you need is a land line. (Cell phones have poor reception and shouldn't be used.) Feel free to wear your bunny slippers.

There's a third strategy for reaching the press, prospects, and spiders that I want to cover in this chapter. It's not for everyone. However, more business professionals could benefit by using it. I'm talking about webinars.

Insider Insights: David McInnis

David McInnis, PRWeb's founder and CEO, pioneered search engine optimized and direct-to-consumer press release distribution strategies.

Photo: David A. McInnis, CEO, PRWeb

What's the #1 mistake marketers make with press releases?

Most marketers think more is better. Aim for 300–500 words. Longer press releases tend to wander, lose cohesiveness, and over-hype a product. This is ineffective for retaining reader interest and getting indexed by search engines.

What's your favorite simple but powerful tip?

Take a "disinterested" writing approach. Most press releases are written or heavily influenced by the business owner who sets out to promote his/her product or service. Hype turns a good announcement into spam.

How have press releases helped your business?

We recently announced the availability of TrackBacks, which allows a blogger to notify the PRWeb platform of a comment that he/she made regarding a press release distributed on our system. PRWeb then creates a link from the press release to the blog comment. Within a few hours, we tracked 22 blogs linking to our press release.

Why Webinars Work

A webinar is a Web-based seminar. Conferencing companies such as Genesys, Microsoft, Raindance, and WebEx offer the technology to invite the world to hear and see your message. It's an engaging tool to communicate with partners, employees, investors, prospects, and customers. It's probably easy for you to think of creating content for those audiences. That's why I've put this technology in this chapter, because few companies think about using a webinar to attract media attention.

Many conferencing companies integrate data, voice, and video over a Web browser such as Microsoft's Internet Explorer. You create the presentation and invite an audience to participate. You and your audience will log into the presentation via the Web browser. Typically, each person must first accept a Java plug-in if the conferencing company detects this update is needed. A click on an "accept" button that appears should do the trick. Watch out for webinars that force people to download and install any necessary technologies because it's very possible they won't or can't.

The webinar can be offered in a few different formats. For example, you could create a Microsoft PowerPoint presentation as the visual part of the presentation. Or you could use a Web camera to capture your live image on video to give your webinar a more "in person" seminar experience.

For the audio, everyone could call a conference call phone number, or you could use a microphone and let people listen to you via the Web (computer to computer Voice Over Internet Protocol, also called VOIP).

Inviting the Press to Attend

Let's talk about inviting the press to your webinar and what's newsworthy.

To attend a webinar, people must usually register for it. You could create a "press only" presentation and require that the participants disclose the media outlet they represent. That lets you know who is going to be there. Because many journalists are freelancers, you can't assume their e-mail address will reveal that information.

Here are ideas of webinars that might interest the press:

✦ A preview of a new product or service

✦ A preview of a new survey or research report

+ A preview of a new case study

+ A preview of new how-to tips

Notice a common theme? I highly recommend giving the press a preview of something new you're about to release to the public. By giving them a sneak peek, you're including them in your public relations plan. This is strategic. Journalists want to be the first to break a story. So give them this opportunity.

You don't have to create a presentation exclusively for the press. An educational event for the public will attract the media, too. Your statistics, case studies, and tips will interest the press and public.

Remember to promote your webinar on your site, blog, and e-mail list. Consider writing an optimized press release about it—and perhaps ask your partners to promote it.

Why not launch an online ad campaign? As I mentioned earlier, webinar participants usually register by providing at least their name and e-mail address. You want as many people to register as possible, regardless of whether or not they actually show up. You'll get them on your e-mail list. That's important if your webinar is free.

> + *Tip:* *Just a note of caution—free webinars often have a high "no show" rate. I once taught a webinar through another company that recorded over 400 people registered, yet only about 100 showed up. If registration is required, at least you can follow up with all who registered.*

Q & A Sessions

Another way to effectively use webinars as a marketing tool is to allow the audience to ask questions during your presentation.

Consider using the webinar interface instead of the phone. Through the Web, participants can type in their questions, allowing you to see which questions you'll choose to answer, even giving you a little time to think before you speak. Your participants may post far more questions than you can answer. That's okay. Your answers might make the perfect Web article, blog post, press release, or some other marketable information.

Although Web conferencing technologies offer handy communication features, you might not want to limit yourself to hosting event-driven webinars. Why not create a webinar that's always open? One that doesn't require you to be present?

Viewstream, an interactive media company, created a Flash-based product demonstration for one of its clients. As long as the viewer's Web browser supported Macromedia Flash, no download was required. Because the webinar was always available, the client's sales team focused on closing sales instead of showing the demonstration on a one-by-one basis. In this case, webinar participants weren't required to register. They called the phone number shown during the presentation, if they were interested in receiving more information.

The result? Within 90 days of posting the webinar and launching a public relations campaign to drive people to it, Viewstream's client saw a 200 percent increase in its lead-to-sale ratio. In case you were wondering if webinars really work as a sales tool, not just a marketing one, I hope this example is reassuring.

Unfortunately, webinars aren't spider friendly. Last time I checked, spiders can't log in, listen in, or watch a presentation. Plus, these are usually hosted on the conferencing company's site, not yours, which means your site couldn't get credit for the content anyway.

Want to know a solution to this problem?

If you can host the webinar on your site, create a special landing page for it. Then optimize that page for relevant keywords. You'll need content. That's where writing a title and summary for your webinar is helpful. Spiders and humans can read that.

Press releases, Internet radio, podcasts, and webinars are all effective ways for achieving online publicity—from the press and prospects. Regardless of which strategies you use, keep in mind that the press will follow the trail back to your Web site.

Unfortunately, many companies forget about the media when it comes to their Web site. If you feed the press with the kind of information they need, you'll greatly increase your chances of being featured.

Feed the Press

An online press center is critical. Because journalists are always on deadline, by publishing important information on your Web site, you'll save them research time while also increasing your chances of being featured in their story.

Your online press center can be one Web page or several pages, depending on how much information you put on your site.

Online Press Center

You can certainly create a "Press Center" section on your site. Or you could post press information in your "About Us" section because journalists know to look there, too. Here's key information journalists will be thrilled to find on your site:

- Brief history of your company including the year it was established (or a business bio if you're a consultant promoting a personal brand, not a company one).
- Names of key executives and a brief bio on each would be a bonus.
- High-resolution images, photos, and logos.
- Past and current press releases.
- Statistics, surveys, case studies, and a sample tips list published by your company.
- Name, date, and link to (if possible) other mentions in the media.
- Awards and reviews your company has received.
- Events calendar of where you may be speaking or exhibiting.
- Contact information, including phone number and an e-mail address, not just an online form, in case it doesn't work.
- An invitation to subscribe to your company's e-zine, or blog feed, to receive timely and relevant information about your business and industry.

Posting this information on your site does two things. First, this boosts your credibility as an industry leader, which shows why you should be quoted as an expert. Second, journalists can quickly find stuff they need to quote you without contacting you.

I go a little crazy sometimes playing phone tag with business professionals or waiting around for their responses by e-mail, when I'm on deadline for my articles. And to be honest, when I'm considering featuring companies I'm not familiar with, I review their Web sites. I look for content that shows credibility. Knowing that, how does your online press center measure up to those of your competitors? Take a few minutes to find out.

An online press center is an essential part of your online publicity plan. It can win or lose a shot at fame.

Missed Opportunities

A rather well-known company lost the opportunity to be interviewed in my *Entrepreneur* magazine column because I couldn't find contact information on its Web site. The online form didn't work either. I even went to Network Solutions to look up contact information, but it wasn't available. Sigh…oh well. Too bad for them.

Another company missed an opportunity because the company didn't put their fantastic survey on their site. I spotted their statistics from the survey on a blog and followed the link to the company that published the survey. It wasn't referenced anywhere on the site. Arg. Although I contacted the company, by the time I received the survey, my deadline had passed, and I had turned in the article without that great information.

If you don't have an online press center, put that on your to-do list. If you have one, take a few minutes to review it and see how it can be improved for the press. The good news is that prospects, potential partners, and investors could be persuaded to do business with you based on this information.

You probably don't want to optimize your online press center for the spiders because these pages aren't likely the most relevant landing pages for your site. A landing page is often the first point of entry into your site. First-time visitors could be better served by landing on your home page or an even more relevant site page that better matches their keyword search. Still, if your online press center gets some press in the organic search results, that's not so bad.

As you'll see from WebTrends' "Success Story," broadcasting the right message at the right time generates big buzz on the Web. This requires a little planning, which is well worth the effort.

Success Story
WebTrends Inc.

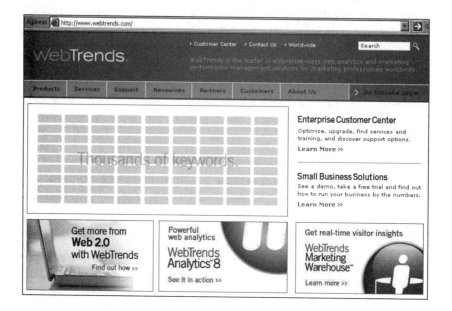

URL: www.webtrends.com

Contact Name: Doug Alexander

Title: Director of Creative Services

✦ Goals/Challenges

What were your specific goals for doing a webinar?

WebTrends' goals for the conducting the webinar "Marketing with Confidence" were to educate marketers about the growing need for better accuracy in Web metrics due to industry research findings, and to drive interest in and leads for the newest version of WebTrends Web analytics solutions (version 7.5), which offered best practices for accuracy.

What challenges/concerns did you face implementing the campaign?

In mid-March 2005, JupiterResearch (now JupiterKagan) reported a decline in the accuracy of cookie-based measurement. Two months later, we delivered the webinar in which we unveiled WebTrends' research that showed third-party cookie blocking had grown fourfold in 2004, expanding the current industry dialogue beyond cookie deletion to third-party cookie blocking or rejection. We also introduced the latest version of our Web analytics solutions that enabled our customers to use first-party cookies as the default, virtually eliminating cookie rejection.

✦ Strategy

Describe your implementation strategy.

Cookies can be a technical topic, and therefore our audience needed to understand the business impact, while others would need more technical resources. This was part of the reason we created different communications from the webinar, including a confidence report, press releases, and a technical how-to guide for implementing WebTrends' first-party cookie solution. We needed to show the severity of the issue while providing an easy solution and clear next steps.

How long did it take to launch the webinar?

The webinar itself took a total of 80 hours from three people over three weeks.

What problems or surprises did you encounter, and how did you resolve them?

After the webinar, there was a high demand for additional information and a short turnaround time. So, after the webinar and unveiling of our research, white papers, and a new version of our Web analytics solution, we had to immediately communicate results of the survey we offered during our webinar and subsequent research reports.

✦ Results

What results did you achieve?

The Marketing with Confidence webinar received 22 percent more registrations than our next most successful webinar, which at the time had surpassed attendance records for any recorded conference powered by Microsoft Office Live Meeting. Our Accuracy Business Brief white paper offered at the end of this webinar has been viewed more than 10,000 times, while our follow-up Web Marketing Confidence report has been downloaded 5,900 times. In additional to generating high-quality leads and sales, we also generated a tremendous amount of press coverage, including two high-profile articles in *The New York Times* and *The Wall Street Journal*.

What's your #1 recommendation for marketers wanting to use webinars?

Use an integrated approach—PR, advertising, marketing—with customer challenges as the focus.

Tips to Remember

Before broadcasting your message across the Web, brainstorm story ideas. Answer the questions "Who cares?" and "Why now?" in your content. Then turn this content into press releases, topics for Internet radio shows or podcasts, and possibly a webinar.

By broadcasting a message instead of pitching your product or service, you'll invite journalists to share your story. They'll take your message far beyond your existing client base. And you can leverage broadcasting channels to simultaneously attract search engine spiders and new customers, too.

Online public relations is about sharing information and building relationships. A "buy now" approach doesn't usually work. This is the perfect job for online advertising. Part II of this book reveals strategies for attracting profitable customers, while also appealing to the spiders and press.

II

Making Online Advertising Profitable for Your Business

6

Connecting
Through E-Mail

Growing your e-mail list is the most powerful and profitable Internet marketing strategy (although getting subscribers to your news feed is becoming a close contender). With a click of the Send button, you can instantly broadcast your message to subscribers who *want* you to contact them. What's better than that?

Marketing to your own e-mail list, when done right, is really a blend of advertising and public relations. It's advertising because ultimately you're selling something. That's why this chapter is in Part II. Yet, it's public relations when you offer valuable information that is not part of your sales pitch. This advertising/PR combination helps you connect better with your e-mail subscribers and create a community of fans that will boost your business. Sadly, many business professionals focus mistakenly on getting new traffic while forgetting to maximize an e-mail strategy that easily pays off…over and over again.

Think a newsletter is your golden ticket? Not anymore. Simply offering an *e-zine*, short for *electronic magazine* and often referred to as an online newsletter, is not nearly as effective as it was in the past. Let's face it—Internet users are sick of spam, and they're overwhelmed by their own daily e-mail communications. So they're no longer subscribing to every interesting e-zine.

Adding to these challenges, more companies and consultants offer an online newsletter now. How often are you invited to sign up? I've been asked at retail stores and at my chiropractor's office. I've even been signed up to e-zines after I've handed my business card to people who asked for it, which really peeves me. (Don't do that. That's spam, not guerilla marketing.) The marketing of e-zines online and offline is increasing.

Even offering free information, a product, or service in exchange for a first name and e-mail address isn't a surefire way to get your e-mail list to explode. I'm not saying these tactics don't work. They do. Just understand that like us, other people are more carefully guarding their e-mail Inbox, too.

Today, more than ever, you've got to communicate the *value* of your free offer. Then you must continue to deliver value in every e-mail you send. This is how to turn subscribers into fans. Who better to rave about you than your fans? Your fan base is bigger than you think. It could include prospects, investors, journalists, students, future and current employees, and even Internet hobbyists, not just customers.

Your fans will promote your business in their e-zines. And they'll mention your URL on their Web sites and blogs, boosting your buzz, as well as your link popularity.

Again, who loves links? Spiders do! While crawling the Web, they'll find these links, which add to your site's expert status. Expert sites are rewarded with higher organic search rankings.

In this chapter, I'll reveal chief ways to make invisible e-mail campaigns visible to spiders. But first, I'll discuss optimizing your e-mail list for your human audience, which should always be your first focus. The search engines contribute greatly to your online visibility. However, spiders don't impact your bottom line—people do.

Creating Your Community

Most Web sites aren't communities. Sure, you can offer helpful information and hope visitors will return. But most won't. That's why a majority of business professionals are committed to a never-ending struggle of getting new traffic. They're not doing anything to create a long-term relationship with visitors.

A blog is closer to being a community. That's because a good blog is continually updated with content, posted by the publisher(s) and readers. It's more engaging than a site. However, without offering your blog posts as a feed so they can be delivered to opt-in subscribers, you must also hope that visitors return to your blog. Most won't. Not everyone uses a feed reader either.

If you're not inviting visitors of your site and blog to opt into your e-mail list, you're missing a huge communication opportunity. Therefore, use both venues to build your list.

Segmenting Your E-Mail List

Although I'm referring to what seems like one e-mail list, you might want several of them for different purposes. E-mail *segmentation* is the process of organizing your list into segments or categories. Companies such as Cooler-Email, ConstantContact, EmailLabs, and ExactTarget generally offer sophisticated segmentation options, although you can create multiple e-mail lists easily through all-in-one e-commerce solutions such as 1ShoppingCart.com and an eBay Store.

Segmentation enables you to send a different e-mail to each segment because not all subscribers respond the same way to the same e-mail. Besides, it's more effective to send relevant information to each e-mail list anyway.

For example, e-zine subscribers expect, well, your e-zine. And although you could also automatically subscribe webinar participants to your e-zine, that might not be the most effective course of action.

Let's say your webinars focus on industry research. You can connect better with webinar participants by sending them periodic e-mail messages about industry trends, statistics, and your upcoming webinars. By customizing your messages for each e-mail list, you create a stronger sense of community with subscribers.

Go ahead. I know you might disagree with the idea that e-mail creates community. It's a monologue, not a dialogue, right? It's the one-way transmission of information. However, the kind of information you deliver, and the way you communicate your message, helps you connect with your subscribers in a way that your Web site can't.

Involve Your Readers

With that in mind, why not invite subscribers to submit questions or comments? Then you can use this feedback to create content for your e-mail broadcasts. This saves you massive time by not having to respond personally to each person. Plus, you serve your subscribers better by sharing in-demand information with them. What a fun way to let them participate. You also show your subscribers that you're listening to them.

The popularity of blogs shows us that people want to participate in a conversation. That's not the sole reason why blogging has taken off, yet it's a significant factor. Creating a community is the next generation of e-mail marketing.

Business professionals can't continue broadcasting information or offers they *think* are important to their subscribers. They need to *know* what's important to their subscribers.

Remember Pete Nelson, CEO of Everywhere Marketing and his "Success Story" from Chapter 2 in this book? He sent a survey to his e-zine subscribers and discovered that 86 percent wanted to know how to set better goals and plan their marketing efforts more effectively. Two months later, Pete wrote an article about this topic that landed him a $145,000 project. He listened to his community.

Rather than guessing, wouldn't you like your subscribers to tell you how you can best serve them?

Instead of asking your subscribers to e-mail their questions or comments to you, you could organize their responses more effectively through an online survey tool such as QuestionPro or Zoomerang. A survey tool is certainly a more time-efficient option if you have thousands of subscribers who are eager to give you feedback.

You can offer your subscribers a list of options to choose from. Their responses are easily tallied up. Also consider offering an open "Comments" field. You'll get answers that will surprise you. Then you can send your e-mail subscribers information they told you is valuable to them. You can refer to a related product or service at the end of your message. If you do this, use a call to action as Alexandria Brown has done in her byline in this chapter's "Insider Insights." See how she invites you to get her free report? Well done. This simple step leads to more business.

Although some press people will opt into the free information you're giving away to attract prospects, consider inviting the media to join a separate e-mail list customized for them. In the event you're not offering company news via a news feed, and to keep in touch with press people who aren't yet using a feed reader, you can create a separate e-mail list to send them statistics, case studies, and how-to tips they may find newsworthy. Journalists might not want to receive your e-zine if it's sent too often; they might prefer periodic updates from you instead.

Regardless, if you manage one e-mail list or many, you'll create a bigger impact and leave a lasting impression when you stop speaking in a corporate voice. Go ahead, get personal.

Get Personal

Before you jump to any conclusions here, let me explain. By getting personal, I mean expressing a personal voice. Let your e-mail seem like a conversational letter. You may have heard the expression, "People do business with people, not companies."

This probably makes perfect sense to consultants who are already doing this. However, even retailers who send out a "Special Offers" newsletter could include a short greeting written by the company owner or executive. This gives e-mail a personal touch. By feeling connected to the author of the e-mail, subscribers become more connected with the company. It's a smart tactic for increasing immediate business as well as brand awareness.

Let me show you a fun example of an online newsletter from one of my clients, Fire Mountain Gems and Beads.

Subject Line: St. Patrick's Day BEAD Sale!

Dear Beading Friends,

Follow a rainbow of colorful gemstone beads and save a "pot o' gold." Many of these great beads are special buys we've tracked down just for you: hard-to-get gemstones like Forest Green and Poppy Jaspers and vibrant Peach Moonstone, as well as unusual shapes like faceted teardrops, hourglass, and dogbones. Most are available only from Fire Mountain, and in limited quantities—don't be left out!

Did you miss the last e-mail special: Spring Fever Saving?

Happy beading from all of us at Fire Mountain Gems™ and Beads.

Chris and Stuart Freedman

This is friendly, right? Great tie into the St. Patrick's holiday, too. This is certainly more personal than a plain "Beads on sale. Buy now" message. Write as though you're *talking* to your subscribers, not *writing* to them. This approach helps you keep a conversational tone.

"Dear Beading Friends" is a better greeting than "Dear Customer." However, use name personalization whenever possible. Seeing "Hi John" is a more personal touch. If your e-mail management program can automatically insert the subscriber's first name into the greeting line, use this feature.

And use a person's name (and title) in your signature line, not just the company name. Every time I get an e-zine from a big company and it comes from the president, I notice—even if a marketing manager probably wrote it. I can't help thinking that I'm actually hearing from the company president. Your subscribers might assume the same.

Chris and Stuart Freedman, the founders of Fire Mountain Gems and Beads, occasionally mention their travel adventures searching for unique gems and beads around the world. What a personal way to introduce new products.

Want another idea? You can also tie into current events to share a personal story. Just a quick note, before your main message, to give your subscribers an inside peek into who you are as a person.

For example, during the winter Olympics, when I shared my near-death experience surviving skeleton training in my e-zine, subscribers instantly replied to either tell me I was cool or insane. A 63-year-old grandfather, new to Internet marketing, wrote a 350-word e-mail sharing his personal and work experiences. Among other things, he told me his son is an extreme sports enthusiast, too. His response made my day.

Getting personal allows subscribers to get to know us. Sharing, not simply selling, is a more advanced e-mail marketing practice.

The personal-style e-mail works for a press e-mail list also. Consider leaving out personal stories. Instead, write a few sentences summarizing the content included and why you believe it's important. Include strong opinions (maybe listed as bullets for easy reading), knowing journalists may use these to quote you in their story.

For instance, start by stating that your company's new survey shows a change in current trends. Include a key statistic or two. Add a bulleted list of opinion statements about the survey data. (These can come from a company spokesperson or survey analyst.) The rest of the e-mail contains survey results. Again, it's not necessary to create a separate e-mail list for the media. It's just a bonus idea.

> ✦ **Tip:** *Warning: It isn't generally a good idea to make the e-mail author a nonexistent person. Once I called a company and asked to speak to the person who had sent me the e-mail. My request caught the receptionist off-guard. There was no such person. I was transferred to someone who informed me that the author of the e-mail was a fictitious character. Oh. I felt embarrassed, and a little tricked. Maybe the company used a nonexistent person to track people's responses to the e-mail. Or perhaps because a fictitious character can't quit, he can always be the online company representative. Interesting ideas, although a real person is often better. If you do use a fictitious e-mail author, remember to tell your customer service team about him…but never tell your customer.*

Remember to brand your e-mail with your logo, tagline or byline, URL, and other unique identifiers. This carries a consistent message to your subscribers and to anyone else who is forwarded your e-mail.

Also subscribe to several e-mail lists to stay on top of your competitors. Which e-mail messages are memorable to you and why? Your competitors are great resources.

Don't see list building only as a direct sales opportunity. It's a big benefit, but the wrong approach. Instead, think about cultivating a community of fans. Sharing valuable information and special offers in a personal voice is the start of a long-term relationship with them. Continue to refine your e-mail marketing strategy because it's a whole lot easier and less expensive to create business and buzz from loyal fans than from first-time site visitors.

Now, let's talk about timing.

Timing Is Everything

Do you let your opt-in subscribers know how often you'll send them e-mail *before* they sign up? You should. If you don't, you're not getting as many subscribers as you could.

Always protective of my e-mail accounts, I don't trust companies' opt-in forms that don't tell me how often they'll e-mail me—no matter how fantastic the free offer looks. I know my e-mail address will be used, and I want to know how often.

Chances are, your potential subscribers do, too. Eliminate their fear of being inundated by e-mail. If you don't, angry recipients who feel they didn't opt into as much communication as you're sending them could report you as a spammer instead of, or in addition to, unsubscribing.

A few years ago, I was asked to write a featured article for the first issue of a company's new e-zine. My byline and Web site URL would be included. I was so excited; the publisher had over 100,000 opt-in subscribers. But later I discovered they weren't direct subscribers. They were on another Web site that invited them to opt into newsletters from "partners." When the publisher sent out the first e-zine, there was no reference to the original site where subscribers had signed up. As a result, the publisher was smacked with spam complaints. I was caught in the crossfire.

Fewer than ten people reported my article as a spamvertisement, yet my site was immediately shut down for 24 hours. Not a good day for me. I could share several lessons about that experience; however, I hope my story shows how serious being labeled a spammer, even unfairly, can be for your business. If people give you their e-mail addresses, tell them how and when you'll use them. And make sure people know they're opting into *your* list, no matter where they're signing up for it.

Privacy Policy

This is a good time to tell you to post a privacy policy. Reassuring potential subscribers that you won't give out their e-mail address increases your opt-in rate. You can keep it short and sweet. Something like "We never sell or share your information with outside parties" works.

And never make people register for a login and password to subscribe to your e-mail list. That's probably the worst e-mail marketing mistake you can make. I still catch companies doing that. Make joining your e-mail list quick and painless.

A Timely Schedule

So, how often should you send e-mail to your list? That's up to you.

Three of my favorite industry e-zines are delivered at different times during the month: the general industry newsletter is monthly, the case studies newsletter is weekly, and the statistics newsletter is daily. Honestly, I cringe at joining a new e-mail list that is broadcast weekly or more often. I'm on info overload as it is.

However, some marketers swear by e-mail frequency. If you go this route, keep your e-mail messages pretty short. Otherwise, an e-mail publication that is too long and too frequent risks a high unsubscribe rate.

Don't let the idea of maintaining constant communication with your subscribers scare you from growing your e-mail list. Start with a quarterly schedule; then move to monthly mailings as soon as you can. You can always increase your communication when you're ready. Just remember to tell your subscribers before you do.

Definitely send something of value to subscribers as soon as they opt in. I'm not talking about a confirmation e-mail, although that's important. What I mean is that you shouldn't make them wait days, weeks, or months to get your next scheduled e-mail. Give them something right away: a free report or your current issue of your newsletter, for example. At the time they subscribe to your e-mail list, they're interested. By sending them something they can enjoy right now, you welcome them into your community, give them another reason to look forward to your next e-mail, and maybe even persuade them to do business with you that day. An effective timing schedule starts with the very first e-mail you send.

One last note about timing. You never know when subscribers are ready to buy from you or interview you for a story. Perhaps something you write strikes a chord with them immediately. Or perhaps months later they realize a need and sift through your previous e-mail messages to find a possible solution. This is why routine communication is critical.

Want a stampede of sign-ups? All you need is the irresistible offer.

The Irresistible Offer

People are probably already opting into your e-mail list. That's great news. But how many aren't? As I mentioned in the beginning of this chapter, simply offering free stuff won't get your e-mail list to skyrocket. People are guarding their e-mail accounts against spam and information overload. You need to eliminate their concerns by communicating the value of your free offer.

Let's first talk about what free kinds of information you can offer. Even though your e-zine is free, consider giving a bonus gift to new subscribers as an incentive to sign up. Remember, an online newsletter itself is no longer a novelty on the Web. An additional offer could persuade first-time visitors to sign up before they leave your site and quite possibly never return. Here are a few examples of free information you could offer:

+ E-book or special report
+ Technical white paper

- How-to article(s)
- Research study or survey
- Audio lessons or podcasts
- Webinar or presentation slides
- Online tool(s)
- Resources list

Godiva currently offers "My Recipe Box," which allows members to keep track of their favorite recipes and dessert ideas. Members also receive Godiva's monthly recipes by e-mail. Hallmark offers free e-cards to members who sign up. Several colleagues and I offer a "Top 10 Mistakes" kind of report. What would work for your business?

You could also tie your free offer to a shopping incentive. For example, when you currently register for Borders' Rewards program online, you can choose one of three shopping discounts as a sign-up bonus. That should encourage new members to complete the sign-up process!

In my quest to find a few international examples, I surfed travel-related sites for about an hour to no avail. Because travel is a highly competitive industry, I wondered why there weren't more of these companies promoting a shopping incentive to grow their e-mail list? An agency or resort could offer a percentage or dollar amount discount for first-time customers.

> ✦ *Tip: If you're offering a shopping offer, set a time limit on it. Creating a sense of urgency often persuades people to take action right away.*

Once you've got people on your e-mail list, you're set. The trick is getting people to sign up. Partner with like-minded companies and consultants to promote your free offer to their list and vice versa. Direct your PR and advertising campaigns to a Web page that in addition to the primary action you want people to take, encourages them to get on your e-mail list as well. And finally, make sure that spiders can see it.

Insider Insights: Alexandria Brown

Alexandria Brown, "The E-zine Queen," publishes the "Straight Shooter Marketing" e-zine. Get her FREE REPORT, "3 Secrets to Publishing a Money-Making E-zine," at www.BoostBizEzine.com.

What's the #1 mistake marketers make with their e-zines?

Making it all about themselves. Make at least 75 percent of your content useful information for your target market readers. The rest can be self-promotion—all about you, your business, your services, and products.

What's your favorite simple but powerful tip?

You'll build better readership and get increased response by publishing more frequently with less content in each issue, versus less frequently with more content.

How has your e-zine helped your business?

Publishing my e-zine has built my business's biggest asset: a targeted and growing list of more than 18,000 prospects and customers, which brings me up to $100,000 in sales each and every month. With ongoing access to this audience I've created, I'm practically guaranteed ongoing income as long as I continue to deliver quality information and resources that are targeted explicitly toward them. (That's why I'm so passionate about teaching e-zine marketing!)

Maximum Exposure

Okay, I've talked about using e-mail to connect with prospects and the press. What about search engines? E-mail marketing is certainly the most challenging strategy to optimize for the organic search results. That's because spiders can't get on your e-mail list. They'll never see your juicy e-mail content or help people find it. That is, unless you make it spider friendly.

Are you ready to discover three easy ways to make spiders grow your e-mail list for you?

Ditch Your Squeeze Page

A *squeeze page* is a page designed to get people on your e-mail list. Usually, the dangling carrot is something free. There's typically a headline, benefit(s) of the freebie, and an opt-in form (requesting at least a first name and e-mail address). And that's it.

Knowing what you do now, what's the monumental problem here? Exactly—no content for spiders. Most squeeze pages are deadly.

More and more, I meet business professionals who have been told to use a squeeze page before giving people access to their Web site, blog, article library, seminar information, and all kinds of great spider bait. Are they crazy?! They've cut off one of the biggest benefits of the Web: *free traffic from search engines.* If you or someone you love has this kind of squeeze page, warn him immediately.

You can kiss press opportunities goodbye. A squeeze page blocks journalists' access to valuable information. They won't go through the effort of opting in. When wearing my journalist hat, there's no way I'd give up my e-mail address just to get access to content that may or may not be quality. Forget it. I'll surf the open Web.

Or Use a Squeeze Page Effectively

Want a squeeze page that builds your list and doesn't kill free publicity opportunities? Then follow these guidelines:

+ Don't hide all of your valuable content behind a squeeze page—only a part of it. Absolutely keep your primary site and blog public. Use a squeeze page to give people access to an exclusive report, discount, or something extra special.

+ Use your visible content and particular marketing campaigns to drive people to it. A squeeze page can be a powerful marketing tactic, but don't destroy your online publicity potential by burying all of your valuable content behind one.

Use Featured Articles as Bait

People join your e-mail list to get something of perceived value. That's why you shouldn't give away all of your good stuff on your site or blog. You need to save something special as an incentive to join your e-mail list. Here's a simple solution to getting people to join your e-mail list while also getting free exposure on the Web.

Choose a few popular keywords. (Refer to Chapter 1 for a refresher on creating a keyword theme.) Write several articles based on the keyword(s) assigned to each article. Within the article's content or byline, invite readers to get on your e-mail list to get your valuable free offers.

Bingo! Spiders will find these and now, so will humans. Plus, your well-written articles persuade readers to join your e-mail list.

Expose Everything

If you publish a ton of information, or constantly launch new products/services, don't hide these gems from the Web world.

You might not be concerned about sharing all of your information. Actually, your visitors could be overwhelmed. They might want to join your e-mail list to get highlights. Therefore, you have another option. You can use e-mail to send subscribers to the Web.

In your e-mail, include top headlines, teaser copy, and URLs that link to your article pages or product pages. This lets you optimize more content for the search engines because these Web pages are publicly available.

Be sure to invite people to join your e-mail list from multiple pages of your site, such as article and product pages, not just the home page. This goes for your blog, too.

Many visitors enter your site from another one of your site pages. If your e-mail opt-in form is only on the home page, you'll miss getting a whole lot of people on your list. Many business professionals don't realize this. Today's e-mail subscribers are tomorrow's customers. So give the invitation to join your e-mail list top visibility across all your pages. Here are a few ideas of where to invite people to opt in:

✦ As an opt in box within a header at the top of a page; people can enter a first name and e-mail address right there.

✦ As an opt-in box within the content of a page; people can enter a first name and e-mail address right there.

✦ As an op-in box within your main navigation area; people can enter a first name and e-mail address right there.

✦ As a clickable menu option from within your main navigation, which could take people to a special page with more information about joining your e-mail list.

✦ As a promotional box or banner within the content of a page, which could take people to a special page with more information about joining your e-mail list.

✦ As a clickable link within the content of a page, which could take people to a special page with more information about joining your e-mail list.

One of the biggest mistakes I see business professionals make is forgetting about their e-mail list. They focus exclusively on sales. That's short-sighted. Many people will buy something from you or feature you in their story much later. It's all about timing. Your e-mail is their reminder. That is why building your e-mail list is critical.

Throughout this book, I focus on prospects and the press as the most important human audiences. Understandably, they might not be the only two audiences you want to reach.

For instance, people marketing a nonprofit organization can optimize their Internet strategies to attract donors and volunteers. If you're a representative from a nonprofit organization, then the following "Success Story" is especially for you. Don't skip it if you're working in the business world. One of the reasons I chose the World Wildlife Fund was to share its fun, creative approach to building an e-mail list while educating their community. Business marketers and nonprofit marketers can learn from each other.

Success Story
World Wildlife Fund

URL: www.worldwildlife.org

Contact: Matt Finarelli

Title: Manager, Online Marketing, WWF U.S.

✦ Goals/Challenges

What were your goals for your e-mail marketing campaign?

Our overall list-building goal was to increase our e-mail list size by 50 percent each year (knowing there's about a 30 percent subscriber churn rate). As part of our overall goal, we created a campaign for people to help suggest the name of a pygmy elephant that WWF scientists were going to be radio collaring in the field in Borneo.

What challenges/concerns did you face in implementing it?

The main challenge was to let people know that we had an online newsletter. Getting people to sign up was the next challenge. We only wanted opt-in subscribers—no list rentals or data dumps—people who cared about WWF's mission.

✦ Strategy

Describe your implementation strategy.

Not only was this a fun game for people to play, but it was also a great way to educate our members about this newly discovered subspecies of Asian elephants. All along the way, we asked for participants to sign up for our e-newsletter.

How long did it take to launch your campaign?

Because we have a great Web team, we were able to launch from scratch in about two weeks. The main delay was making sure our field team actually had collared the elephant!

What problems did you encounter, and how did you resolve them?

We needed to record everyone's submissions and votes accurately (including time of entry since we were going to award the prize—a plush pygmy elephant—to the person who sent us the winning name first). We also consulted our legal department about the rules for this contest. And finally we had to make sure that our form captured e-mail addresses of people who entered their suggestions or votes, and yet allowed them to choose not to opt into our e-newsletter if they didn't want, while being also compliant with the Children's Online Privacy Protection Act.

✦ Results

What results did you achieve?

After phase 1, we added over 800 new e-newsletter subscribers from 3,000 game participants. Phase 2 brought in another 300 new subscribers from more than 4,500 participants. When we released the winning name (*Penelope*), we asked the participants to help support our conservation efforts to protect pygmy elephants by making a donation. The results were startling. Contest participants returned a net income/e-mail of almost eight times higher than the rest of our e-newsletter list. We gained over 1,000 new newsletter subscribers who are very interested in helping WWF and had elevated the profile of pygmy elephants to all of our online members.

What's your #1 tip for e-mail marketers?

Bring people in through some sort of engagement. These e-mail campaigns perform much better than those that simply say "sign up for our e-newsletter."

Tips to Remember

Grow, grow, and grow your e-mail list to create a community of fans.

Give them an irresistible offer for signing up. And while giving them high-value information and special offers, get personal. Include stories that give you, and your company, a unique voice in the noisy Web world.

Just don't hide all of your valuable information behind spider-blockers such as squeeze pages. No, no, no. Give your e-mail campaign maximum exposure by using delicious content to bait spiders, as well as humans.

Want a shot of instant visibility across the Web that'll bring in new business? Reach out to affiliates, your performance-based marketing partners.

7

Unleashing an Affiliate Force

Affiliate marketing is pure performance advertising. Affiliates are partners who promote your business by linking to your site, and they are paid for the results they achieve. (Amazon.com is an example of a merchant who supports a huge affiliate force.) You pay affiliates for clicks, leads, or sales. Or any combination of these. Who wouldn't want to pay only for guaranteed results?

Top affiliates are some of the savviest marketers on the Internet.

They have to be. Their success determines their income. They're battling against your competitors to win consumers' business for you. And they're competing against the other affiliates in your program. If affiliates want to eat, and eat well, they must stay on top of the cutting-edge tools and techniques that will make both of you money.

Watch out. Affiliates could be spammers. In their quest to deliver instant traffic to your site or blog, some of them will spam. They'll send e-mail spam. Ever receive unsolicited e-mail from a big brand? Very likely, the merchant isn't spamming you, but their affiliates are.

When left unchecked, you could suddenly find yourself having to deal with affiliates gone wild. They're spamming your brand and burning your reputation all over the Web.

Affiliates often focus on search engine optimization because it's a highly converting strategy. Good affiliates play by SEO rules. Spammers will use "churn-and-burn" domains to promote your business and then do blog spamming, or other spam tactics, to get their domains to the top of the rankings. Your site could be penalized for their bad behavior because these pages direct search engine users to your Web site. Your business is obviously benefiting from the spam. Search engines see this.

Don't worry. There are plenty of ethical affiliates. The good they deliver far exceeds the bad possibilities. They'll boost your business as well as your company's buzz and brand awareness, which can get the media's attention. Using a spider-friendly management program gives your company an extra dose of visibility. This is all part of an effective affiliate strategy, which I'll cover in this chapter.

By taking time to plan your approach, you'll develop an incredibly powerful marketing team who will leverage their expertise for your business as long as you take care of them. Good affiliates are golden.

Think about Amazon again. The company launched its affiliate program in 1996 and today has over one million affiliates. I bet you wouldn't mind one million people promoting your company, would you? A significant part of Amazon's success can be credited to its affiliates. Amazon is a great example of how unleashing an affiliate sales force can build your brand online while also bringing you significant business.

You might even be an Amazon affiliate, or an affiliate of another merchant's program. I am. Being an affiliate is an easy way to generate passive income. In this chapter, I'll not only cover how to successfully manage your affiliates, but also how you can add additional income by becoming one.

Affiliates: Friends or Foes?

Many merchants launch an affiliate program without a plan. Dangerous move.

You're putting your brand into the hands of Internet marketers who could burn it quite quickly. You could also lose your best affiliates by not adequately supporting and rewarding them. In this section, I'll reveal the most important decisions you need to make to create a successful affiliate marketing strategy.

The first question you need to answer is: *What's your policy on channel conflict?*

Channel Conflict

Channel conflict refers to competing with your partners in the same space. This concern was raised years ago when manufacturers went online and started directly competing with their own resellers for new customers. Many Internet-savvy resellers complained, of course. With bigger marketing budgets and brand recognition, parent companies could dominate the Web and steer business away from their resellers.

Some manufacturers responded by using their Web sites to provide information but not sell anything. They directed prospects to their local reseller instead.

Some manufacturers started direct selling online but supported their resellers in ways that helped them sell more online too.

Other manufacturers essentially said "too bad" and started selling online anyway.

Today, channel conflict is a hot topic for most companies that plan to launch an affiliate program or already have one. Their biggest concern is the search space.

Search Marketing Conflict

Do you really want to fight against your competitors *and* your own affiliates for top organic rankings? There's no guarantee that your site will outrank your affiliates' sites. If their sites do outrank yours, you'll pay them for directing search engine users to your site. But if these consumers find your site first, then you don't pay an affiliate fee. Maybe you should restrict affiliates from doing search engine optimization.

What about pay-per-click? Oh yes, affiliates do that too. PPC adds an additional problem to channel conflict with your affiliates: *Your click fees will increase.* I've seen this happen where soon after my clients launch an affiliate program, their per-click fees skyrocketed because they started bidding against their own affiliates.

I know what you might be thinking. But it's not a good idea to let affiliates do PPC as long as they don't outbid you. First, many will anyway. Second, the major search engines are using a ranking model that considers advertisers' ad quality score along with advertisers' maximum bids. Basically, this means your affiliates could bid less than you on a keyword and still outrank you in the paid search results.

Wait. Don't cut off affiliates from search marketing...yet. There's another way to look at this situation.

Your affiliates, even if their sites outrank yours, are filling up the organic and paid search results with links that ultimately direct people to your business. Isn't it better that people find your site instead of your competitors' sites?

Besides, because search engine marketing converts like crazy, affiliates will likely leave if you prohibit them from doing it. They could head straight to a competitor. Would you be willing to pay a performance-based fee if that means you'll have a bigger, more aggressive marketing team promoting your business all across the Web, including search engines? That's something to think about.

Trademark Marketing Concerns

To add one more level of complexity to this sticky situation, what about trademark marketing? There's a difference between marketing keywords relevant to your business and marketing your trademarks.

For example, "The London Landmark" is the hotel's trademark. As the name of the hotel, these words identify the owner. It is part of the hotel's brand, whether it's a government-registered trademark or not. Keywords such as "London hotel" and "luxury London hotel" are relevant, yet more generic than trademarks.

Some companies prohibit their affiliates from promoting their trademarks in the search space while allowing them to promote relevant, or generic, keywords. Why?

Because many merchants feel they've invested significant time and money generating brand awareness for their trademarks. They want people searching for these brand keywords to be directed to them, not passed through their affiliates who are cannibalizing their marketing efforts.

Look at travel-related search results to see this problem in action. Search for the name of a hotel. Often, the hotel's site isn't even on the first page of search results! This is a problem because some people won't type your URL into the Web browser; they'll look up the name of your company, product, or service in a search engine.

Trademark marketing is critical for companies with brand awareness. Will this be your task, your affiliates', or both?

Just a note about pay-per-click: If you encourage your affiliates to do PPC, or if you want to do this as an affiliate, check out the search engines' site ownership rules first in their editorial guidelines. A search engine could require that affiliates do the following:

+ Use their company's name in the ad copy, not just the merchant's name.
+ Submit sites they own; they cannot directly link to the merchant's site using their affiliate URL.
+ Brand their Web site with their company's contact information, not the merchant's information.

Savvy affiliates want to work with merchants who don't restrict their income potential. If you're putting restrictions on the search space, include these in your affiliate agreements and communicate your policy because many won't bother reading the agreements.

The more complex your restrictions, the more you'll have to police your affiliates. For example, if you prohibit them from doing PPC but allow them to do SEO, then you should routinely check paid listings and send violators a warning or two before you kick them out of your program. Don't be too hasty about this.

I've talked to affiliates who get upset by merchants who only contact them to reprimand them. Some affiliates aren't aware of your policies, or they forget them. It happens. They're super busy promoting other merchants. On the other hand, some violate your policies because they can.

A recovering spammer told me he didn't care about merchants' brands or their policies. When cut off, he'd focus his spamming efforts on other merchants. Whoa. His attitude illustrates the importance of properly managing your affiliate team.

Although I've focused on the search space in this section, channel conflict can happen with other Internet marketing strategies, too. If you haven't addressed this topic yet, put this on your to-do list immediately.

Depending on the policy you create, your affiliates can be powerful friends on the Web. Or they can be foes that compete with your own marketing campaigns and profits. It's not their fault if they're foes. It's your responsibility to create your policies and communicate them to your affiliate team. This is absolutely essential if you plan to join an affiliate network or are already in one.

Instant Networks

Are you wondering how to instantly build an affiliate force? Then join an affiliate network like Commission Junction, LinkShare, or Kolimbo.

Networks give you access to thousands of eager affiliates. Being a merchant in a network gives your affiliate program speed and power. Sounds perfect, right? Well, an affiliate network isn't for all merchants. With speed and power can come problems, especially depending on how much control you're given over your affiliates through a network. I'll explore the chief advantages and disadvantages in this section.

Advantages

Okay, clearly the biggest benefit of joining an affiliate network is connecting immediately with a huge number of affiliates. You won't need to sit around hoping they find your "Join Our Affiliate Program" page on your Web site. You won't need to seek them out either.

In a network, your offer is immediately available to affiliates who are ready to work for you. Many will race to promote your business before other affiliates do. Affiliates make more money if fewer of them are promoting your business. So, new merchants attract attention. That is, if their offers are competitive.

The biggest mistake you can make initially is to join a network and not do competitive research. You need an appetizing offer, or nobody will promote your business. Here's what you can do. Sign up as an affiliate first—it's free. You can then scout out your competition to come up with a better offer.

For example, if a hotel marketer sees that his competitors are offering five cents a click to affiliates who deliver traffic, he should offer more. I know I said a new merchant has instant appeal because nobody is promoting his offer yet. True.

However, the two questions every affiliate wants answered are: *"What's your payout?"* and *"What are your conversion rates?"* New merchants don't have conversion rates. Because of that, affiliates will compare your payout to the payout and conversion rates of your competitors. Show affiliates they can make more money with your program.

Another advantage of a network for merchants and affiliates is the easy payment system. You pay the network, and they distribute payments to affiliates. If you manage your own program, you'll need to cut checks to each affiliate, or use affiliate software that includes a check-writing service or bank-deposit service.

Let's look at how speed and power can create problems.

Affiliates Gone Wild

Never ever let your affiliates run wild. Although this is a bad idea when you grow your own team too, the problem is amplified in a network environment thanks to the sheer number of affiliates who could instantly rush to the Web to promote your business. Some will spam.

Thankfully, networks are responding to this growing problem by creating better tools for you to manage your relationships.

For example, you can screen individuals before you accept them into your program, contact them directly concerning their tactics, and kick them out if necessary. Yet, you still must monitor your affiliates because even when kicked out, spammers might reapply to your program under another identity. And surprisingly, spammers could be your best performers.

As you'll read in this chapter's "Success Story," Custom Direct discovered that one of its affiliates who was generating thousands of dollars a month in business for their company was a spammer. They immediately kicked him out.

Not only will removing spammers from your program protect your brand from being further burned online, but you'll also be supporting your ethical affiliates who were competing against the spammers. Give your heroes more of the money they deserve!

Even though I referenced clicks as a possible offer for a hotel marketer to use, as opposed to leads or sales, be careful with this model. It might attract more Internet spammers than the other two. Affiliates who are paid on a per-lead or per-sale basis are forced to deliver quality traffic that converts. Affiliates who are paid for clicks don't worry about quality. Because your brand reputation and organic search listings are in the hands of thousands of Internet marketers, you must patrol your affiliate community constantly if you're paying them for traffic. Spammers' short-term tactics can become your long-term headache.

Tracking Links

Speaking of search engines again, are you wondering if affiliates boost your site's link popularity? That depends.

In the early days of affiliate networks or software, the answer was no. That's because the URLs your affiliates used were not *direct links* to your Web sites. The root domain belonged to the network or software, which then redirected to your Web site URL.

There are two problems here. First, to improve your link popularity the root domain must be **www.yourcompany.com** and not **www.affiliatecompany.com**.

Second, what's wrong with redirects? Yup, spiders hate them. Redirects are now considered spam. Click a URL from a site that links to yours and watch the URL in the Web browser. If the underlying domain switches to another URL, it's a redirect. No link popularity points for you.

There's good news. Whether you join a network, or use software to grow your own team, the links given to affiliates to promote your business might now use your root domain name in the link. (Kolimbo offers this feature.) Hooray!

Okay, this isn't a real link, but for simplicity's sake, let's pretend a spider-friendly link for one of your affiliates is **www.yourcompany.com/aff=1**. See? Your root domain is there. That's good for spiders.

Unfortunately, the direct link can be good for bad affiliates. If your root domain is being used in their search engine spamming efforts, your site could be at higher risk of being banned by the search engines.

This doesn't mean redirects protect your site from spammers. Not at all. Your site is still obviously the one benefiting from your affiliates' bad behavior. Direct links are at a higher risk of associating your site with spamming tactics of naughty affiliates.

Improving your link popularity, and subsequent search engine rankings, is a benefit of using an affiliate network or software that uses direct links.

But if you're using an affiliate management solution that works well for your business, don't change it now! You can launch a link popularity campaign instead. Changing from one set of marketing tools to another is almost always a tedious process. You'll want to avoid that unless necessary. On the other hand, if you're ready to launch an affiliate program, or you've had it with the solution you're using, consider programs that offer a direct domain linking feature.

Affiliate software may be better for you than an affiliate network. Software is generally a lot less expensive. Plus, you might prefer to grow your own hand-selected team. This could be the way to go if you want to avoid same-channel conflict, especially in the search space.

Homegrown Teams

Besides cost, the biggest advantage of a homegrown affiliate team is summed up in one word: *control.*

I'm not saying you don't have control over affiliates if you go through a network because you do. It's just that the instant unleashing of such a massive force can create massive management problems. A homegrown team has its advantages.

Benefits of Hand Selecting Affiliates

First, if you promote your affiliate program to your community of prospects and customers, then you're connecting with people who are familiar with your company. Many are already fans. Who will probably promote your business better: strangers or fans?

A stranger can say "I've heard company X is good." Whereas a fan can say "You've got to call company X. Their [product/service/newsletter] helped my business grow by 25 percent in one month!" Easy decision, right? Fans make better salespeople than strangers.

I'm an affiliate of Internet tools that I've used for my clients' marketing campaigns. I mention these in my e-zine, blog, and Web site. Although I'll recommend tools that don't offer an affiliate program, it's nice to get a commission. It's like the merchant is saying "Hey, thanks for promoting us, Cat." I appreciate that. Inviting your community to become your affiliates is a way to thank your fans for raving about you.

Affiliates who are fans also raise the media's awareness of your superstar status. When your colleagues praise your company in their marketing materials, that can be newsworthy. Journalists watching your fans can now hear about you from them. That's an advantage of leveraging an affiliate strategy to reach the press too—greater exposure. Hand-selecting your affiliate team and using management software can help.

Affiliate Management Software

AffiliateShop and DirectTrack are examples of software solutions (and both offer direct domain linking). As with many Internet marketing tools, affiliate management software has become pretty sophisticated, and I don't generally recommend that companies invest the time into building their own custom solution.

Besides, now affiliate software companies might offer an affiliate network (and vice versa). What a convenience. If growing your own team isn't going fast enough, you can tap right into their network. That's a handy option.

Did you know you might have a free option at your fingertips?

E-commerce solutions such as 1ShoppingCart.com and Yahoo! Merchant Solutions offer an affiliate-tracking feature in their advanced packages. (Neither offers direct domain linking at this time.)

Their affiliate feature isn't typically as advanced as the software programs or networks dedicated to affiliate management, but they're free. And they're a breeze to use because they're already integrated with your shopping cart. Less "techie" might be more attractive to you. An all-in-one solution from 1ShoppingCart.com and Yahoo! Merchant Solutions is a low-cost, time-efficient option for business professionals who want one easy-to-use tool set to accomplish multiple marketing tasks.

Perhaps the thought of suddenly managing hundreds or thousands of affiliates seems overwhelming. And that's why you decide to skip networks for now and instead hand-pick your team members.

Start by reaching out to a small segment of your community, like customers. Want a bigger team? Invite your newsletter subscribers and blog readers to join. And definitely contact consultants and companies that have their own fans. These are *influencers*. They can ignite buzz, brand awareness, and immediate business for your company.

By offering an affiliate relationship to influencers, you'll also avoid channel conflict. Do you see how? Instead of inviting affiliates to promote your business all across the Web, you're selecting where and how your business is promoted by hand-selecting your affiliates. Talk about total control.

And because they've created their own community of fans, influencers are profitable partners. No channel conflict and high performance are a great combination.

Finding affiliates isn't your final goal. The performance of your affiliate team comes down to your communication with them. By helping your affiliates achieve greater success, you'll contribute to your own.

Insider Insights: Declan Dunn

Declan Dunn is CEO of DunnDirectGroup.com, one of the most successful marketers on the Internet. He has launched FunMoneyGood.com, a Podcast network driven by affiliate marketing.

Photo: Declan Dunn, Dunn Direct Group

What's the #1 mistake marketers make with affiliate marketing?

Not paying affiliates on time! The source of power is affiliates, not affiliate software. There are no second chances to win back high-performing affiliates who are working hard marketing your business online.

What's your favorite simple but powerful tip?

Develop a relationship with your affiliates. Communicate with them often, offer bonus incentives for reaching performance goals, and keep control while being personal and accessible.

How has affiliate marketing helped your business?

I set up my first program offering my book, which launched a huge affiliate program and a multimillion dollar agency within one year...the power of affiliates is amazing.

Communication Is Key

Imagine a highly successful sales team that works for you. They can recite your company's values and competitive advantages in their sleep. They can't wait to tell others about your product or service. And best of all, they continue to bring in new business quickly and easily. They're well-informed, motivated, and effective.

How does a dream sales team get this way? Luck? Nope. Think you could hand them your company's marketing materials and then disappear until the annual sales meeting? Not a chance. A successful sales team needs training and motivation. An affiliate team is similar to a traditional sales team. If you want them to perform well, communicate with them.

After interviewing dozens of merchants, I believe the optimal communication plan includes three phases: *introduction, education,* and *motivation.*

Phase I: Introduction

The first phase is introducing your affiliates to your program and company. It's the training period. This actually starts before they sign up because you'll need to share the essential info to persuade them to enroll.

Tell them what they'll be promoting, how much you'll pay them, and when they'll be paid. Once they enroll, give them details on your program policies, as well as sample copy and graphics they can use to promote your company, products, or services. Giving them this information helps them ramp up their efforts quickly and easily. Your affiliates will appreciate that.

Plus, giving them content to use right away reduces the chance they'll use your site's content. What happens if they create a Web page that looks exactly like one of your pages? That's right—duplicate content. That's search engine spam. You don't want that. Protect your site's organic rankings by telling affiliates they can't simply duplicate your site's content, and by offering them high-converting sales copy to use instead.

Phase II: Education

Phase two, education, starts soon after affiliates join. And it continues as long as they stay on your team. Continually send affiliates information to help them perform better. Keep them updated on changes to your products or services, and the associated offers, too.

For instance, a hotel might let affiliates offer a $50 spa credit to encourage prospects to make a room reservation. The hotel should let affiliates know in advance that a $50 breakfast credit will replace the spa credit. And also tell affiliates when they should change their marketing materials to coincide with the hotel's new offer.

Also share advanced selling tips with your team as part of your educational process. Let's say a hotel discovers that the copy "Soak Your Stress Away with Our $50 Spa Credit" performs better than the "$50 Spa Credit with Your Stay" copy. Why not share this information with your affiliates? This helps them make both of you more money.

Invite feedback and questions also. I've heard from a handful of affiliates who contacted merchants with questions, only to be ignored by them.

Um, if your salespeople have questions on how to better promote your business you wouldn't tell them to go away, would you? Of course not. Surprisingly, several merchants treat their affiliates that way. Hopefully, those affiliates will soon work for you instead.

Phase III: Motivation

Phase three is the bonus round: *motivation.*

Your affiliate communication plan might already include an introduction and education. That's great. Want to help your affiliates achieve an even higher level of success? Offer them performance incentives.

I've spoken to affiliates who get offered cash, gift certificates, even cars. You could offer an award to affiliates who reach specific performance goals. Or you could create a monthly or quarterly contest that rewards the highest performing affiliates. Believe it or not, your performance incentives don't have to cost a fortune.

One merchant I spoke to once offered plasma screen televisions to his top affiliates. Yes, I know those things aren't cheap. Hold on for a moment. The interesting thing about this story is that those affiliates made such gigantic sales commissions every month that they could have easily bought dozens of plasma screen televisions themselves. The merchant said his affiliates couldn't stop chatting about trying to win them at their offline affiliate retreat. He was shocked.

Why was it a cool contest, do you suppose? Exactly, it was a contest.

Your affiliates may be motivated to earn a bonus incentive or win a contest for being "the best." Don't assume that money is the only motivational factor. It doesn't have to be.

What's a Good Payout?

Talking about money, merchants who are launching new affiliate programs might be wondering what's a good payout? The range is wide open.

I've seen merchants offer as little as a few pennies per click and as much as thousands of dollars for a sale. Informational products and services tend to have much higher payouts because they cost less to produce than a manu-factured item or customized service. This isn't always the case, but it's a good generalization.

As a merchant or affiliate, don't get caught up in percentages.

For example, a 50 percent sales commission sounds impressive, but what if the product or service is selling for $10? How many affiliates will work their magic on the Web for only $5 per sale? Not many, I imagine. On the other hand, a 10 percent sales commission on a $1,000 product or service is $100. Much better, right?

As I mentioned earlier in this chapter, do competitive research to determine your affiliate payout. Join an affiliate network as an affiliate to check out competing offers. And browse your competitors' Web sites to see if they talk about their affiliate program there.

Affiliate marketing is profitable for both merchants and affiliates. As a business professional, you're in a prime position to generate additional passive income as an affiliate. It's the easiest Internet marketing strategy you can use for an instant revenue boost.

Cross-Selling as an Affiliate

Optimize your Internet marketing campaigns for maximum sales, status, and visibility, and you're in the perfect position to become an affiliate. You've created a community that wants to hear from you. Tell them about the resources that will help them, and you'll also help your own business.

By becoming an affiliate, you can create additional revenue instantly without creating what it is you're promoting. You'll promote another company's product or service and receive payment for every visitor, lead, or sale you deliver to the merchant's site. You're not responsible for creating the product or service or delivering it. That's the merchant's job. Whew. All you need to do is recommend the merchant to your online community and include the unique affiliate link you're given, which tracks the number of clicks, leads, or sales you generate.

You can include your affiliate link in your e-mail broadcasts or e-zine. You can post it on your order confirmation page. You can use it on your company's Web site or blog.

There is no exclusive arrangement between merchants and affiliates. You're free to promote more than one merchant at a time. But be careful as to who and how you promote as an affiliate.

The "Who" of It

Let's talk about "who" first. Being an affiliate means you're recommending another company's product or service. Have you tried what the merchant is selling? What reputation does the merchant have? Your own credibility is on the line when you promote another merchant as an affiliate. Choose consultants and companies that are closely aligned with yours.

First, this means they should offer a product or service that makes sense to your community. Using my hotel example again, a hotel could be an affiliate of a nearby spa if it doesn't have one at its hotel. That relationship makes sense.

Second, the hotel and spa should be closely aligned in terms of brand image. For example, a five-star spa is a good match for a five-star hotel. They appeal to the same audience. This affiliate relationship will work well while supporting the hotel's brand image.

The "How" of It

Now, the "how." Don't distract your community from doing business with you.

Unless you are first and foremost an affiliate, then make sure you're not sending business away to other companies. It's never a good idea to promote another merchant on your home page, shopping cart pages, or in other areas that can convince your community to stop their interaction with your business to go someplace else. You'll not only lose those immediate sales, but you'll miss getting them on your e-mail list, which means you'll lose future sales as well.

Earlier in this section, I mentioned how you could promote merchants on your Web site. A "Resources" section of your site is an ideal place. An order confirmation e-mail or Web page is even better because at that point, customers already have bought something from you anyway.

The Impact of Affiliates

Declan Dunn's "Insider Insights" shows how a consultant can leverage affiliates to catapult into superstar status, while Custom Direct's "Success Story" at the end of this chapter shows how affiliates can be chief contributors to a company's bottom line.

Years ago, I bought checks from one of Custom Direct's check companies that donated a percentage of the sale to a nonprofit organization I wanted to support. Before I reordered checks months later, I noticed very few check companies at the top of the paid and organic search results did *cause marketing*, which is a marketing partnership between a company and nonprofit where the nonprofit is served in some way. One of Custom Direct's check companies won my business again.

Not only did I want to share Custom Direct's affiliate marketing "Success Story" with you, but I chose this company because of its commitment to the community. There are many ways we business professionals can serve our communities, and I see cause marketing as an underutilized marketing strategy on the Web. Perhaps this story will give you more than one marketing idea.

Success Story
Custom Direct LLC

URL: www.cdifund.com

Contact: John C. Browning

Title: President/CEO

✦ Goals/Challenges

What were your goals for your affiliate marketing program?

We wanted to drive sales to our 11 personal and business check companies, including Message!Products and ClassicChecks through which we give a percentage of our sales to nonprofit organizations.

What challenges/concerns did you face implementing the campaign?

Time was our biggest concern. We were worried about an affiliate program being worth it. And we were concerned about the time needed to manage affiliates and deal with spammers.

✦ Strategy

Describe your implementation strategy.

By using My Affiliate Program by Kowabunga Technologies, we can tap into their screened network of affiliates who are ready to work. Reading their handbook made the implementation process pretty painless.

How long did it take to launch your affiliate campaign?

About three months from the planning stage to launch. The actual implementation and testing took about one month.

What problems or surprises did you encounter, and how did you resolve them?

At a conference, we learned that an affiliate in our network was a spyware spammer. Although that affiliate made several thousand dollars for us, we kicked him out anyway. We were surprised that we didn't lose as much revenue as we thought we would. Apparently, that affiliate was also stealing other affiliates' cookies and getting the credit for their sales. By kicking out the spammer, we helped all of our ethical affiliates. It's important to stay on top of your affiliates' activities.

✦ Results

What results did you achieve?

The first three months following our program launch, our affiliates generated an extra $3,000 in new revenue for us. In month four, our affiliates generated over $11,000 in just 30 days. Two years later, our affiliates are now responsible for bringing in over 4 percent of our online revenue.

What's your #1 recommendation for affiliate program merchants?

Routine communication. Just like your sales team, they need training and support to make you, and them, more money. One of our most successful affiliates says we're her most responsive merchant. Our new affiliates get daily and then weekly e-mail from us for eight weeks after sign-up, to get them up to speed on our program. And all affiliates receive our monthly affiliate newsletter. We also offer a monthly newsletter and respond to their questions. Communication is key.

Tips to Remember

You'll have a tough time finding employees and marketing agencies that will work on a performance basis. There's a group of savvy Internet marketers who are up for the challenge: *affiliates*.

You can tap into an instant network, or grow your own team. Take a little time to create your program policies and communication plan to help your affiliates maximize their performance. Their success is your success. And become an affiliate to add additional revenue to your bottom line. Both sides are part of a powerful affiliate marketing strategy.

You might encourage your affiliates to play in the pay-per-click space, or you might prohibit them from being there. It doesn't matter who is marketing your business there, but someone should be. Regardless of what you might have heard or experienced with the PPC side of search, it is still profitable as long as you learn how to avoid the potholes. I reveal chief ways to protect your PPC profits in the next chapter.

8

Maximizing Pay-Per-Click

Pay-per-click (PPC) is one of the fastest and most profitable ways of reaching a highly targeted audience online. It'll also bleed you dry if you're not paying attention.

Most search engines show organic listings and paid listings on the same results page. Paid listings are almost always on top. This is a benefit of being an advertiser; your ad is seen before the organic listings. This prioritization of ads shouldn't be a surprise. After all, the search engines don't make money off their free listings. (Well, they actually do if the top-ranked pages display their paid ads. More about that in the next chapter.)

Paid listings are typically PPC ads. In this program, you choose and bid on keywords relevant to your business. These days, you can often get started for just a $5 account activation fee. There's also a cost-per-click fee.

Although the program's minimum bid per keyword could be as low as $0.01 per click, don't expect to pay this. If the search engine uses a quality score, a system for measuring the relevancy of ads, your required minimum bid could be significantly higher. Also, competitive keywords are pricey. That's because advertisers are trying to outbid each other for top spots.

Years ago, most PPC programs were bid-to-position. The highest bid got the highest position. Not anymore.

Following the money-making model of Google AdWords, some search engines offering PPC now use a ranking algorithm to determine which ad gets the highest position. Your bid is only one factor. Other factors can include your ad's click-through rate, the relevance of your ad copy, the historical performance of your ad, and even the quality of your landing page. (A *landing page* is the Web page that people "land on" after they click your ad.)

Microsoft's Live Search ad program, which is powered by Microsoft's adCenter, uses a ranking algorithm. So will Yahoo!'s Sponsored Search, whose bid-to-position model should be replaced by a ranking model by the time you read this book. Your ad's rank is important because generally the higher your position, the more clicks you get.

Unfortunately, the search engines won't reveal every factor in their algorithm. Nor do they reveal the weight of each factor. However, your click-through performance is critical. The search engines say consumers decide your ad's relevance by clicking or not clicking on it. I can see their point.

However, an ad-ranking model that rewards advertisers who get more clicks certainly boosts the search engines' bottom line. But your goal isn't clicks, I'll bet. You want customers (or a goal beyond traffic). That said, don't mistakenly chase clicks. Instead, focus on *conversions*, desired actions that occur once people land on your site (or blog).

With so much competition these days, is pay-per-click still profitable? *Yes.* At least, it can be.

In this chapter, I'll cover two profit-boosting strategies that a majority of advertisers don't maximize. These can be used to win over press and spiders, as well as new customers. I'll also uncover the growing dark side of PPC that has a lot of advertisers anxious—click fraud.

The good news is that PPC isn't limited to the search engines. It has become a popular advertising model on the Web. Many Internet Yellow Pages, directories, and content sites now offer it. There's even better news for advertisers: PPC has evolved.

Today, local-only businesses have better targeting options through local search. And companies that can close more business by phone instead of over the Web can choose a pay-per-call program. I'll cover the highlights of both programs in this chapter.

Let's start with an unusual approach to PPC. Advertisers are obsessed with instant sales, as they should be. Watching sales skyrocket within one month, seven days, or even within 24 hours can turn advertisers into PPC addicts. But be careful. By obsessing over immediate sales, you're missing a huge opportunity.

PPC as a PR Tool

First, the bad news.

You're losing a lot of money on PPC.

To an extent, it doesn't matter how much you fine-tune your keywords, ad copy, or landing pages. You should be following these procedures routinely, as optimizing your campaign for maximum performance is critical. By doing this, you'll greatly increase your profits. The problem is, no matter what you do, some people just aren't ready to do business with you today.

Now, the good news. There's a simple solution. Get people who click on your PPC ads on your e-mail list; or get them to subscribe to your blog or podcast feed. This is one way to use PPC as a public relations (PR) tool.

If you're using these communication channels to educate subscribers, build your brand, and develop a relationship—that's PR. A majority of advertisers don't think of using this approach with PPC. Yet growing a community of prospects does ultimately bring in new business. If you're trying to sell something, that's advertising.

Persuade People to Opt In

I'm not suggesting that you stop selling products or services to get people to opt into your community. Not at all. You can use PPC to sell something, yet at the same time persuade people to opt in. This maximizes your PPC profits. That's because today's prospects are tomorrow's customers. And journalists who stay connected with you are more likely to feature your company. Here are a few ideas to consider:

+ **Feature your opt-in offer on your landing page.**

    Always send people to the most relevant page in your site for your PPC ad. This increases your sales and PPC profits. On this page, make sure your opt-in offer (i.e., newsletter or blog/podcast feed) is clearly visible. Don't distract visitors from doing business with you. Just feature your offer in case they want to opt in before, or instead of, buying something at that time.

+ **Highlight your opt-in offer throughout your site.**

    Unless you remove your site navigation from your landing page(s), people will surf around. So don't put your opt-in offer only on your landing page(s). Highlight it throughout your site. This consistent exposure can persuade visitors to opt in before they buy something or before they leave your site. (Ask customers to opt in during, or after, completing their purchase, too.)

+ **Promote your opt-in offer in an exit pop-up.**

    Even though some marketers swear by them, I hate pop-ups. A disruptive ad that suddenly blocks the information I'm trying to see usually annoys me into leaving the site. Some search engines will reject your PPC ads if you use a pop-up on your landing page anyway. However, an exit pop-up can pass the search engines' editorial guidelines while also persuading visitors to opt in as they're leaving your site. It's the perfect time to say "Before you go..." and offer them an appetizing offer they can't refuse.

Squeeze Pages

Be careful using a squeeze page for PPC. This is a page designed solely to collect contact information, such as a first name and e-mail address. A PPC ad that sends people to a squeeze page that lacks adequate content will be rejected by the search engines, or it will get a poor quality score, which means your minimum bid will skyrocket.

If you're going to use a squeeze page, include the following: relevant content, information about your free offer, a privacy policy, and company contact information. You may also be required to link to your site or blog, or link to a site map, which is a Web page that shows links to your site or blog. Although squeeze pages can work for PPC, remember they're bad for SEO (see Chapter 6 about this). Use them strategically.

Enticing the Media

No discussion of public relations is complete without talking specifically about the media. They're checking out PPC ads, too.

When I'm wearing my journalist's hat, two reasons compel me to interview PPC advertisers for my articles. First, the organic search results are often polluted with junk affiliate or ad-publishing sites. Because I need to interview merchants, not affiliates or ad publishers, I can't stand wasting my time going to sites littered with text ads and pop-ups. Yuck. Not all affiliate and ad sites are this bad, but the bad ones offer no redeeming value to journalists.

Second, I figure the companies willing to spend money on PPC ads are "legit." That's an assumption, I know. But so far, I've found several solid companies this way. A click that leads to being featured in the media could be worth a whole lot more than getting a customer. Not that you need to choose one or the other. Both audiences will see your ad. And inviting journalists to opt into your community is one way of hooking them.

> ✦ **Note:** *Want to know a secret PR tactic?*
>
> *Consider launching a PR-specific PPC campaign. A handful of savvy corporate marketers are already doing this.*
>
> *Here's what you can do. Bid on industry buzz words, write an ad promoting your free information, and direct journalists to a landing page about this topic. Offer stats, case studies, or tips—the stuff journalists want. This is an innovative way to reach journalists who are researching story ideas.*
>
> *Hopefully, your competitors haven't thought of this yet. A couple of companies are even using PPC to respond to a PR crisis. For example, a company slapped with a lawsuit could bid on its company name followed by the word "lawsuit," which would direct the press*

to a landing page about the company's side of the story. Because not responding to a PR crisis can be a problem, why not respond to it through PPC? Quite possibly, your PR nightmare is being talked about on other Web pages that are being ranked in the organic results. A PPC ad can help you diffuse the fire that's being fueled in the organic results.

Launching a PR-specific PPC campaign is an advanced strategy. It's okay if you're not ready for this yet. You might be soon. It's important that you know about it now.

PPC can be a profitable PR tool, not just a direct sales tool. But to achieve your goals, whether they include publicity or sales or both, you must optimize your landing pages.

Optimizing Your Landing Pages

As I mentioned in the last section, you should be tracking the performance of your keywords and ads. The wrong keywords can kill your campaign. And bad ad copy attracts browsers, not buyers.

Fortunately, many PPC advertisers are diligently refining their keywords and ads. Unfortunately, few are optimizing their landing pages…everyone else is wasting money.

Landing pages hold the key to your profits.

That's because without spending more money on traffic, you'll get more of your visitors who "land on" the assigned Web page to buy something (or opt in).

This doesn't just mean your revenue will increase. Your profits will explode. And if you direct other online and offline marketing campaigns to the landing pages you use for PPC, you'll increase your revenue and profits from all of your campaigns. The benefits reach far beyond paid search.

The best landing page for your ad is the one that's most relevant—a category page or product page, for example. Choosing the best page is an essential start. Once you have at least several weeks of PPC performance data, you can start testing new landing pages.

While there are limitless changes you can make to your landing pages, they fall into one of three categories: text, graphics, or layout. Text includes the words used in headlines, descriptions, body copy, image captions, and testimonials, for example. Graphics can include photos, artwork, and illustrations. Layout options include font size and style, colors, the placement graphics and text, and combinations of these various design elements.

You don't have to test these all at once. In fact, you shouldn't. Not if you want to know which elements make your sales and profits spike. My colleague made two text edits to his landing pages that resulted in an additional $90,000 in sales within 30 days! That's motivating, isn't it?

While you can make changes and track them, like my colleague did, you may prefer to hire an eye tracking company. Companies such as Auragen Communicatons, Eyetools, EyeTracking, and the Nielson Norman Group use focus groups to track what people see and don't see. Your report could show that people read your headline and then stop. Or perhaps they bounce around looking at photos, never seeing your "Buy Now" links.

To save money, start by testing one landing page. Choose a Web site (or blog) page that gets a lot of traffic. And choose a landing page that is a model for your other site pages. If you apply your winning formula to Web pages that rank well in the organic search results, you'll catapult your profits from SEO.

Wait. Did you catch that? You can use PPC to drive traffic to, and test, landing pages you'll want to optimize for organic rankings. Why do SEO on a poorly performing page? The free traffic it gets will be worthless. PPC can change that. That is, if you want spiders to see your landing pages, maybe you want to block them.

Excluding Spiders

Does the idea of blocking spiders seem strange? I can understand that. Especially because throughout this book, I reveal how to attract spiders to improve your visibility on the Web. Yet sometimes, it's best to keep your landing pages a secret.

Here's a perfect example. Let's say for 30 days you test three special offer landing pages through PPC (`www.company.com/ad1.html`, `www.company.com/ad2.html`, and `www.company.com/ad3.html`). Nobody on your Web site can see them because you don't link to them. Only people who click your PPC ad will land on them. Or so you assume.

Spiders crawling your site will find them. What happens when these PPC-only landing pages show up in the organic search results? Uh oh. The whole Web world sees them. Not good if you only want your PPC audience to get this deal.

Worse, what if you stop offering this deal but forget to remove these pages from your server? Even though your PPC ads no longer link to them, people surfing the organic search results find them. And they get ticked off when they try to get the special deal, but your company says that the offer is no longer valid.

Don't let this happen to you. Hide the landing pages you're testing through PPC from spiders—and hide the pages you don't want them to find. You might not want spiders finding the landing pages you've created for an e-mail campaign or offline marketing campaign either.

Use the *robots exclusion protocol* to keep spiders out. This is a piece of code that tells spiders which parts of your site shouldn't be accessed. In the top-level directory of your site, create a robots.txt file and put your secret landing pages in it (as well as other pages, folders, and scripts you don't want them to find). Here's what the code of a robots.txt file looks like to block spiders from seeing the aforementioned landing pages.

Example of a Robots.txt File:

User-agent: *

Disallow: /ad1.html

Disallow: /ad2.html

Disallow: /ad2.html

A Webmaster can easily create this page for you. Just tell him which areas of the site you want excluded from roaming spiders.

Want to see what a live robots.txt page looks like?

Go to a Web site (a search marketing company should have this) and type `robots.txt` after the root domain. For example, `www.company.com/robots.txt`. Voilà! There it is.

Ahem…although I've told you this so you can see a live example, I bet you'll use this to see what your competitors are hiding. Go ahead, it's fun.

Let me explain how to do this by using my earlier example of special landing pages you might create. Your competitor would notice **/ad1.html** in your robots.txt file. He'd then add this file name to **www.company.com** into a Web browser like Internet Explorer. In an instant, he'd see your hidden Web page for **www.company.com/ad1.html**. This is a spy trick you'll probably enjoy—when used by you, not your competitors.

On that note, to hide your landing pages from your competitors as well as spiders, put them inside a folder. You could create a folder called "ads," for instance. And then the robots.txt file would look like this. Now, competitors can't see the pages hidden inside that folder.

Example of a Robots.txt File:

User-agent: *

Disallow: /ads/

Don't let the concept of excluding spiders scare you. Give this section of the book to your Internet geek who can whip out this page for you in minutes, sparing you from worrying about it at all.

You can stay focused on improving the profitability of your landing pages.

The "Success Story" at the end of this chapter comes from one of my clients, Fire Mountain Gems and Beads. Jeff Manheimer, the company's Web development coordinator, shares how simply reorganizing the content on one of the company's PPC landing pages turned one of their keywords from a money-loser into a money-maker. One simple step can really make a difference.

There's a dirty secret of the pay-per-click that you've probably heard about by now: click fraud. Since I exposed it in my first book, *Search Engine Advertising* (2004), the topic has exploded in mainstream media, and the search engines are at the center of the bad publicity.

The Evils of Click Fraud

Click fraud refers to artificial or invalid clicks on your ads. It's a profit killer to victims. Yet even with new monitoring tools and lawsuits filed against the search engines, click fraud continues to happen.

The topic of click fraud exploded in 2006. Although it's been going on for years, it has finally grabbed mainstream media attention. In the first quarter, major news outlets reported on Google's $90 million settlement in a class action lawsuit over click fraud. A few months later, Yahoo!'s lawsuit was settled. (The dollar amount was not capped.) These surely aren't the only search engines in hot water, but as the biggest names in this field, they dominate media coverage.

Although this problem isn't exclusive to search engines, for simplicity's sake I'll refer to their PPC programs in this section. There are two click fraud perpetrators I'll cover here: your competitors and ad publishers.

Your Competitors

Your competitors could click your ads to waste your budget, hoping that you'll drop out of the paid listings so they can take your place. Don't panic...yet. The search engines have some click fraud protection in place.

Dozens of data points for each click, such as the IP address of the click, time of the click, repeat clicks, and other click patterns are evaluated. You won't pay for clicks the search engines determine are fraudulent. Not to worry—competitors can't click your ad a hundred times in a row to drain your budget. This kind of obvious click fraud is caught.

Ad Publishers

Your competitors aren't generally the primary threat. Ad publishers are.

These ad publishers can display your PPC ads on their sites or blogs. When this happens, they basically get a commission from the fees you give to the search engines.

Do ad publishers have an incentive to click your ads? You bet they do. Smart click fraud perpetrators create a *clickbot*, software that produces automatic yet random clicks on ads. Even savvier perpetrators create a *botnet*, a network of computers infected with this software that can make fraudulent clicks impossible to catch.

Catching Click Fraud

Fortunately, you can catch some click fraud.

I've spoken to corporate marketers who caught as much as $50,000 a month in click fraud. Unfortunately, the ones I interviewed wouldn't let me share their stories. They're worried that telling the truth will prevent them from getting additional refunds from the search engines in the future.

In a nutshell, you need to study data such as click and conversion patterns by keywords, as well as the IP addresses of clicks. (An IP address is the number assigned to a computer connected to the Internet.) Web analytics can provide this data. ClickTracks, HitBox, Google Analytics (previously Urchin, which Google acquired), and WebTrends are examples of Web analytics. Look for unusual patterns. And routinely monitor your conversions.

PPC bid management tools that track your return on investment (ROI) could be used to identify suspicious clicks, too. I prefer ROI-based bid management tools. These optimize your bids based on cost-per-acquisition goals. Inceptor's BidCenter, Direct Response Technologies' KeywordMax, Omniture's Search-Center, and Atlas Search (previously GO TOAST, which was acquired by Atlas DMT) are examples (Did-it.com is often included in this category; however, this is a service-based agency, not a tool.)

There are also click fraud monitoring tools, such as WhosClickingWho, and service providers, such as Click Forensics and Clicklab.

Don't Obsess Over Click Fraud

Now, I'll say something you might find shocking. *Advertisers with PPC small budgets shouldn't worry about click fraud.*

If you're spending $500 a month, should you waste your valuable time trying to identify if 10 to 15 percent of your budget is possibly at risk? No, you shouldn't.

Too often I hear new or small advertisers complain that PPC doesn't work for them, or that click fraud is wasting all their money. Hardly. In most cases, they're using poor-performing keywords, ad copy, and landing pages. It ain't click fraud. It's their campaigns.

Hopefully, this is reassuring if you haven't yet tried PPC because the media has scared you about this subject. Don't let it keep you from trying this profitable ad strategy. Corporate marketers, listen up.

One of my clients, spending well over $10,000 a month, said her team was too busy to look into it. She called any potential click fraud "a cost of doing business." Um, that's disconcerting. Once you're spending tens of thousands of dollars a month or more, add "monitoring click fraud" to your to-do list. Even a small percentage of waste could be significant.

I can see my client's point, though. PPC advertisers can make a lot more money by optimizing their campaigns instead of focusing on a potential problem that might not even exist.

Why not turn your attention to local search advertising instead of, or in addition to, policing your clicks? It's a great profit-maximizing strategy. Don't skip the next section if you're marketing to a national or international audience. Local search advertising can be profitable for advertisers no matter where they do business.

Getting Neighborly Through Local Search

Some companies need local advertising. Restaurants, car tire shops, massage therapists, and dentists are great examples. If you serve local clients, there's no point wasting your money advertising to people who are outside your target audience. Luckily, your future customers are using search engines, and today you have several ways to reach them cost-effectively.

You've always been able to bid on regionally based keywords. "Los Angeles life coach," for example. Thankfully, searchers have become much more sophisticated users. More people are doing regional searches these days, so you'll reach a great number of ideal prospects (and journalists) by bidding on regional keywords.

Consumers are also including countries, states or provinces, cities, regions, ZIP codes, and other regional keywords in their search phrase. This means you have even more phrases you can bid on. And there's something else you'll be happy to know.

Insider Insights: Andrew Goodman

Andrew Goodman is the founder of Page Zero Media (www. page-zero.com), a search advertising agency. He is the author of Winning Results with Google AdWords.

Photo: Lana Slezic

What's the #1 mistake marketers make with PPC?

This might sound corny, but by not doing it! I hear a lot of hypothetical questions, from people who have never run campaigns, which could be cleared up by just running a test. The other biggest mistake is not paying attention to the landing page and inherent quality of the offer.

What's your favorite simple but powerful tip?

Start with Google's own keyword research tool. It's more powerful than many people realize.

How has PPC helped your business?

I mainly use it for indirect lead generation. I send traffic to an e-book offer, which gets something in people's hands and may lead to consulting services down the road, as well as other opportunities.

Although there are fewer searches for regional keywords than non-regional keywords, regional keywords are usually more profitable. They convert better because they're more targeted.

For example, "life coach Los Angeles" is more targeted than "life coach." Because many life coaches work by phone or e-mail, it really doesn't matter where the life coach lives. Yet according to keyword tools, people search for a local life coach anyway.

Some customers prefer working with a company in their neighborhood. This is why any company (or consultant) can consider local search advertising, even if it serves national and international customers.

Regional keywords are usually profitable because they're also less expensive.

For example, using Yahoo!'s View Bids tool, the current maximum bid for a #1 position on Yahoo! for "life coach Los Angeles" is $0.43 per click. Compare that to a #1 position for "life coach" which is $1.63 per click. (This information is based on Yahoo!'s current bid-to-position ad model, which will be replaced by an ad ranking algorithm by the time you read this book. In December 2006, Yahoo! already stopped making the "Top 5 Max Bids" and its View Bids tool available inside advertisers' accounts.)

Unfortunately, because savvy PPC advertisers are quickly catching onto this profit-boosting tactic, regional keywords aren't always less expensive.

The current maximum bid for a #1 position on Yahoo! for "life coach New York" is currently $2 per click. Nuts. No deal there. If you're lucky and act fast bidding on regional keywords, you could get a powerful and profitable edge over your competitors.

Business directories and Internet Yellow Pages offer pay-per-click programs, too. Business.com and Verizon SuperPages.com are two examples. You can bid on keywords, categories, or sometimes both. The highest bid typically gets the highest business listing position. I can see an ad-ranking model replacing the bid-to-position model here also.

The Geo-Targeting Option

Another way advertisers can zoom in on local customers is through geo-targeting. Some search engines, business directories, and Internet Yellow Pages now offer this option.

In geo-targeting, you'll choose countries, cities, states or provinces, ZIP codes, or possible a regional area in which your ad will be displayed. Consumers are shown ads based on their IP address, the number assigned to the computer connected to the Internet. This isn't their personal computer. An IP address(s) is assigned to the computer servers of their Internet Service Provider. This can cause a problem, which I'll tell you about soon.

Let's say you're a life coach based in Los Angeles, California. You could choose a geo-targeting option allowing only people in the Los Angeles area who search for "life coach" to see your ad. This is a helpful option. Some people will use regional keywords ("life coach Los Angeles") and some won't ("life coach"). Geo-targeting lets you reach the second type of searchers, who are in the geographic area you want to reach. Well, that's what you hope happens.

The problem is that consumers don't always connect to the Web from a computer in the same area they're in. They see the wrong ads. That means you're advertising to the wrong audience.

I ran into this with a client recently. I set her ads to appear to consumers in a few states, including California. She called me in a panic because she couldn't see her ad. I checked, and there it was. Because we were both in California, we both should have seen it. I asked her to describe the ads she saw. They were Canadian! How bizarre. Either her IP address wasn't being detected right, or perhaps the server that connected her to the Internet was in Canada.

IP address targeting isn't perfect. But that doesn't mean you shouldn't try it.

In fact, test regional-keyword targeting and geo-targeting to see which performs best for you. Perhaps both are profitable. As with all online marketing, there's only so much analysis you can do before you try something. Get out there, test a campaign, and track it. Then you'll know.

With the two options, regional-keyword targeting and geo-targeting, local searches can be challenging to grasp. It doesn't help that some search engines, Internet Yellow Pages, and even directories offer programs that are different than what I described here. Check out your country's most popular local search programs to get the options available to you. It's worth testing, regardless of where your business does business.

There's another pricing model that has evolved from pay-per-click that you may want to check out. How about paying for a phone lead instead of for a click? If you prefer to talk to prospects, then pay-per-call is for you.

Converting Customers with Pay-Per-Call

Why pay for clicks when you can pay for calls?

Pay-per-call is the perfect option for companies that prefer to close business by phone. Or, for those which don't have a Web site yet, but still want to advertise their company online for relevant keywords.

FindWhat.com (now MIVA) is credited for launching this program first in the U.S. in 2004, through a partnership with Ingenio, a telephony provider. Since then, pay-per-call programs have popped up all over the Web from providers such as America Online (also powered by Ingenio), Verizon SuperPages.com, Espotting.com, as well as search engines and other advertising-based publishers.

Generally speaking, in a pay-per-call campaign, you'll choose your keywords, possible categories, and the geographic areas where you want to trigger your ad (generally national, regional, or local).

Your pay-per-call ad typically includes a title, description, and a phone number. (A special tracking phone number may be assigned to you that will then redirect calls to one you choose.) If clicked, your ad might link to a full-page informational ad that again shows your phone number.

As you may expect, you won't be paying pennies for a phone call.

The pay-per-call program providers realize you're not getting traffic. You're getting leads, which are significantly more valuable. Therefore, your cost starts at several dollars per call. Some program providers set a flat per-call fee, whereas others let you outbid your competitors. In the second scenario, the highest maximum per-call bid generally gets the highest ad position. As with pay-per-click, because higher ad positions generally get more clicks, the idea of getting a higher number of calls entices advertisers to bid more.

Finally, you may even be charged a monthly service fee, or a per-minute fee, in addition to the other pay-per-call programs fees. Overwhelmed yet?

Not all pay-per-call providers use the same pricing model. And because these are always changing, I can't give a detailed breakdown of who's offering what. That info would be outdated by the time you read this book. My goal is to give you a basic understanding of how it works. Does this seem to make sense for your business? If so, here are a few questions that will help you choose a program that's right for you:

+ What are all the fees for this program?

+ How can I control my costs?

✦ On which sites could my ads be displayed?

✦ Which kinds of calls are charged? (Ask about repeat calls and hang-ups.)

✦ Can I turn my listings on and off to coordinate with my business hours?

For some business professionals, PPC competition has hiked click fees up to a point that a click could cost the same as a call! Would you prefer to pay the same price for online traffic or live leads? I vote for leads.

And because pay-per-call is relatively new in the world of paying for performance online, you'll find higher profits here initially if you beat your competitors to this space. That is, if the pay-per-call program you choose is based on a bidding system. Get dialed in soon.

Remember that while the pay-per-call program providers deliver prospects to your phone, you're responsible for closing the deal. At several bucks a pop, be sure your phone sales team has been well trained to sell. You can't afford to pay for calls that you can't convert into customers.

Depending on the pay-per-call program provider, advertisers won't get the same amount of business as they can through pay-per-click. The PPC providers might reach a lot more Web searchers. You need to test your options. Not to sound like a TV infommercial disclaimer, but *individual results may vary*.

Pay-per-click and pay-per-call could both be profitable for you; maybe one will overwhelmingly outperform the other. You won't know until you test them and track your conversions. You may be surprised what you find out.

Success Story
Fire Mountain Gems and Beads

URL: www.FireMountainGems.com

Contact: Jeff Manheimer

Title: Web Development Coordinator

✦ Goals/Challenges

What were your goals for doing pay-per-click?

We expected a 100% ROI (return on investment) at some point. We were also hoping for greater brand awareness, as well as filling in our exposure where we were not ranked well organically.

What challenges/concerns did you face implementing the campaign?

We were concerned about the time needed to manage the project and bidding wars. Our greatest challenges were categorizing our keywords into ad groups and landing pages, and translating our print CPA (cost-per-acquisition) goal into a Web CPA goal. Fortunately, our CPA from PPC is lower than it is from print.

✦ Strategy

Describe your implementation strategy.

A considerable amount of time was spent on keyword research, ad copywriting, landing page assignment and redesign, and implementation of an ROI-based bid management tool that also worked with our Web analytics program. We also determined a CPA goal that no keyword could exceed.

How long did it take to launch your pay-per-click campaign?

Two and a half months.

What problems or surprises did you encounter, and how did you resolve them?

Some of our keywords failed our CPA target surprisingly fast—within days—and were automatically deleted from our campaign by the bid management tool. Within 24 hours from launch, troubleshooting and optimizing our PPC campaign, and the bid management tool, became a full-time job for the first 60 days from launch. We decided, pre-launch, to commit a part-time person to this, but we quickly realized that to make the most of it we should have a full-time person.

✦ Results

What results did you achieve?

We achieved more than a 100 percent ROI within the first 24 hours and have maintained it ever since. Even better, our CPA is two-thirds less than our print campaigns. And we filled in the exposure gap missing from our search engine optimization campaign.

What's your #1 recommendation for pay-per-click advertisers?

Spend time optimizing your landing pages. Our keyword for "alphabet Beads" failed our CPA goal twice. We realized that our assigned landing page started to list 388 relevant items, then continued on 19 more pages that shoppers had to click on to see. Because we have about 150 alphabet beads, this left a great percentage of the alphabet line unseen on the first few pages. We decided to change the entry landing page to orient the visitor to our four different lines of alphabet beads. And we put the alphabet category options "above the fold." Since we made changes like these, "alphabet beads" has not failed our CPA goal.

Tips to Remember

Due to the increasing competition in the pay-per-click space, advertisers must find new ways to maximize their profits.

First, see PPC as a PR tool, not just a sales tool. A lot of people who click your ads won't buy from you immediately. Or perhaps they're journalists and never planned to anyway. Get them to opt into your community. By doing this, you can build business relationships that last a lifetime.

Second, besides optimizing your keywords and ad copy for maximum performance, optimize your landing pages. Just a few text, graphic, or layout changes make an impressive improvement to your bottom line—not just for your PPC campaigns, but for any campaign that uses those landing pages.

Finally, if you're spending a few hundred dollars a month on PPC, don't worry too much about click fraud until you've optimized other areas of your campaign. Corporate marketers, if you haven't already, routinely should monitor click fraud and document it so they can request a refund.

As additional ways to reach new customers cost-effectively, consider local search and pay-per-call. As fairly new advancements, you can find good deals while competition is low.

There's another part of pay-per-click that's just too big to cover under this chapter, and it has its own set of disadvantages and advantages you need to be aware of. I'm talking about contextual advertising. You might not only want to be an advertiser, but you might also want to be an ad publisher.

9

Reaching Out Through Contextual Advertising

Want massive exposure on the Web without massive upfront work? Contextual advertising may be your answer. Using this strategy, your text or graphical ad can be instantly displayed on hundreds or thousands of Web pages deemed relevant for your ad. Is getting online exposure really this simple? It sure is.

Companies such as ContextWeb, IndustryBrains, Quigo, and Vibrant Media display your ad on sites (and blogs) belonging to their ad publishers. So do several search engines such as Kanoodle, Google (Google AdSense), Yahoo! (Yahoo! Publisher Network), and soon Microsoft.

Contextual advertising is a huge time-saver. You don't have to work with individual publishers. Through one program, your ad immediately appears across a network of sites—some impressive ones, in fact.

Want to advertise on the Web sites of *Entrepreneur, Forbes, NASCAR, Martha Stewart, Golf Digest,* or other big brands that are the perfect fit for your business? These top-tier publishers might not offer online advertising, or they might have costly minimum contracts. This rules out advertisers with small budgets. That's okay, there's another way in.

Contextual advertising is your back door into advertising on sites like these. That's because publishing powerhouses are joining contextual advertising networks to maximize profits instantly from their high-traffic sites.

Even better—instead of a cost per thousand impressions (CPM) model and expensive contract minimum, you'll often find a pay-per-click (PPC) model and usually a $5–$100 minimum commitment. All advertisers can participate.

> ✦ *Note: Contextual advertising isn't new. In the 1990s, ad networks displayed 468 × 60 pixel-sized banner ads across a network of relevant Web sites. This was a more sophisticated targeting option than buying run-of-site banner ads, which appeared on any kind of site. In fact, run-of-site ads performed so poorly that all banner advertising was quickly and unfairly slammed in the media. Yet, keyword-triggered banner ads were very profitable. Today, keyword-triggered graphical ads have even made a comeback, thanks to new ad formats and contextual ad programs.*

Today, contextual advertisers have greater options for targeting ad viewers. For example, you can do demographic or behavioral targeting, both of which I'll cover in this chapter.

Unfortunately, although contextual advertising is evolving, its unique challenges threaten the budgets of unsuspecting advertisers. You're reaching a different kind of audience. Because a lot of business professionals make mistakes with their contextual ad copy, copywriting is covered in this chapter, and so is "the dark side" that can get you into trouble.

And then there's the publishing side of contextual advertising. If you've got traffic, you can easily generate extra, passive income.

Let's start by looking at how contextual advertising works and what you need to do to maximize your online visibility while minimizing your costs.

The Need for Transparency

In contextual ad programs, advertisers often choose the categories (or topics) of sites where they want to display their ad. They might also choose keywords the Web pages must have, or be related to, in order to display their ad. These days, advertisers might even get to choose specific Web sites or Web pages that display their ad.

We can thank the search engines' pay-per-click (PPC) programs for paving the way for keyword targeting and the PPC model, which today is a common pricing model in contextual advertising, as well as other online ad programs.

Don't praise the search engines yet. Contextual ad companies are leading the way in transparency. Search engines, on the other hand, have been dragging their feet.

Worse, they dump their keyword search advertisers into their contextual advertising programs without warning. Yup, you've been opted in. I've seen advertisers bleed money on contextual advertising because they didn't realize they were already paying for it! Let me explain how this happens.

Advertisers—Be Warned!

In recent years, several search engines began offering two types of self-serving ad programs: keyword ads (search network) and contextual ads (content network). My last chapter covered keyword ads, typically referred to as PPC. This is where you bid on relevant keywords, and only when those keywords are searched for is your ad displayed.

In contextual advertising, your ads appear on relevant site (or blog) pages. A keyword search does not trigger your ad. Instead, it's already displayed on the page. Although there are other types of contextual ad formats, I'll focus on text-based ads that appear next to content, for simplification purposes.

Sadly, a lot of PPC advertisers who bid on keywords don't know they've also been enrolled in contextual advertising! Bad search engines. Google (AdWords) and Yahoo! (Sponsored Search) do this, and they're not the only ones. (Kanoodle, on the other hand, deserves recognition for introducing its contextual ad program as a separate program from search. Advertisers must opt in; they're not automatically thrown in.)

You know why the search engines automatically enroll you in contextual advertising, right? Yup—money. By sending you additional traffic, they boost their bottom line. Chances are, this traffic is blowing your budget.

If you're new to pay-per-click, opt out of the content network immediately. I've seen big and small advertisers waste a truckload of money on it.

If you're an experienced pay-per-click advertiser, test contextual advertising when you're ready to manage it as a separate campaign from keyword search. (Google and Yahoo! now let you make separate bids on contextual ads and keyword ads. That's a relief. These two campaigns won't perform the same, so they can't be treated as such.)

Another transparency problem is not being able to see, or control, where your contextual ads are displayed. And because just about anyone can slap ads on his site, you could waste a small fortune on junk traffic from poor-quality sites.

Control Over Ad Publishers

Let's be honest. Some sites are garbage. They're created for the sole purpose of publishing contextual ads (and possibly affiliate links). There's no content, only ads. Perhaps these "ads-only" publishers are even spamming to drive people to these Web pages and tricking them to click on ads. Not good.

Your contextual ad could appear on these sites and blogs. What's the value of these clicks on your ads? Worthless. Worse, publishers who are committing click fraud by clicking your ads are further wasting your money.

Wish you could see who could publish your ad? Want to block specific sites? Thankfully, you're starting to get this option.

Depending on the contextual ad program, you could block, or accept, specific sites from showing your ads. Google gives you several targeting options if you create a site-targeted campaign. But beware: You're still opted into its content network when you launch a Google AdWords campaign.

Site-targeting, or page-targeting, is a very valuable feature. It gives you the ability to customize your own publisher network, which enables you to control your costs and profits better.

Not all contextual ad programs will happily give you this control. Their advertising model is not your business model. You're focused on conversions; they're focused on delivering clicks (or impressions, if that's their ad model). When you're empowered to reduce the number of clicks on your ads, ad publishing networks can lose a ton of money. Fortunately, there's mounting pressure from the advertising community to get greater control over where their ads appear. It's coming.

Even if a contextual ad program doesn't offer site-targeting or page-targeting capabilities, it may offer other interesting options. Perhaps you can target your ideal audience by their demographics and online behavior.

Demographic and Behavioral Targeting

Demographic targeting is getting new attention. Several contextual ad programs now offer advertisers the ability to target ad viewers based on demographic criteria, such as location, sex, age, household income, or other factors. How is this possible?

Well, when Internet users sign up for stuff on the Web, they're often required to fork over this information. Do you use a Web mail account like Microsoft's Hotmail or Voila Mail? Or have you ever registered online for a newspaper such as *The Wall Street Journal* or *The Toronto Star*? Then you answered demographic questions when you signed up. Now those companies can serve demographically targeted ads to you.

Why Now?

Demographic targeting isn't new; it's been around for years. It's getting publicity today because some contextual advertising companies are now offering it; so for them, it's a new feature. And the search engines are getting into this game, too. Soon after Microsoft introduced demographic targeting to its PPC advertisers, Google introduced this feature to its site-targeting advertisers. That's also new.

Demographic targeting isn't without challenges. If you choose this option, you could miss a lot of hot prospects. Not everyone can be reached through demographic targeting. And just how accurate is this data? You know some people lie, or choose the quickest answers so they can race through the registration process. Still, if demographic targeting is a good option for your business, then give it a try.

Is Behavior Better?

It's unfair to mention demographic targeting without mentioning *behavioral targeting*. This refers to showing ads to people based on their Web surfing behavior.

Wouldn't a tax accounting firm prefer to reach people with a history of looking for tax information online? Sure. Chances are, the firm's ad would reach these Web surfers at the right time. These surfers are in research mode. What a perfect branding and sales opportunity; they're receptive to the firm's message.

Behavioral targeting can be effective because you basically follow your target audience around on the Web. This is important because consumers don't surf in a linear way. People zigzag.

For example, a tax firm's prospect might check out tax articles on the Web. Next, he orders flowers online. He then surfs a tax blog and finally heads to a travel blog, where he sees the tax firm's ad.

This example shows the upside and downside of behavioral targeting. The upside is that your ad could be shown to people who have looked for related information, even if they're on an unrelated site or blog when they see your ad.

The downside includes the potential for inaccuracy and privacy concerns. Regarding inaccuracy, what kind of ad should be shown to someone who equally checked out tax information and online florists? Regarding privacy, do consumers fully understand when their online behavior is being monitored and used for advertising purposes? Is this form of advertising an invasion of privacy?

Behavioral advertising isn't a new topic either. It's resurfacing as a hot topic within the search marketing community because the search engines are jumping into this game.

Is your head spinning with all of your targeting options? It's challenging to give specifics about how this stuff works, yet speak in general terms because Internet marketing evolves at lightning speed. Plus, the programs don't all work the same way. Review those mentioned in this book for their specific features and current offers.

Let's move on to a creative contextual advertising tactic you can easily control—your ad copy.

Repositioning Your Ad Copy

In some cases, text-based contextual ads and PPC keyword ads look exactly the same. They both can include a title and a description. They both can consist of the same number of maximum characters.

Hey, why not use your keyword ad as your contextual ad? Because it won't work. Those audiences don't have the same mindset. Your contextual ad copy must be repositioned for that audience.

The Consumer Mindset

Let's look at search engine users. When they type a keyword into a search engine, they're looking for something specific. For instance, "tax accountant." These are hot prospects. You want to attract these people if you represent a tax accounting firm, right? Yes! Therefore, a PPC ad that says "Get an Accountant Who Can Cut Your Taxes by Up to 35%" could hit home with consumers searching for "tax accountant." These prospects will convert into customers real quick.

Now, let's look at people who surf content sites and blogs. Your contextual ad will appear on the tax-related sites and blogs they visit. Do you know if they're looking for a tax accountant? No. They could be looking for free tax forms. Or for free tax tips. What about the history of taxes? Who knows?

Unless your contextual ad program lets you choose the exact pages on which your ad will appear, you won't know the exact nature of the content. For example, your ad could appear on an "I hate taxes" personal blog. (This example again points out the need for transparency and advertiser control. There are some Web pages you don't want showing your ad.)

Although these contextual ad viewers might ultimately need an accountant, you can't hit them with your "Buy Now" ad. Well, you could. But generally speaking, people surfing content sites and blogs are looking for information. A "Buy Now" ad is a turnoff. They're not that far along in your sales cycle…yet.

You'd be better off writing an ad about the free information you're giving away. For example, a "Get a Free 21-Point Tax Checklist" ad works better.

It's going to appeal to a wide range of people seeing a variety of tax topics. Besides, people who want that checklist are probably close to doing their taxes. Your checklist could inspire them to hire your firm instead of suffering through the tedious work of doing tax paperwork on their own. See how writing contextual ads for a general, information-seeking audience can turn into business?

And who else is interested in your free information? Journalists. They're surfing sites and blogs looking for their next story idea. Your "Buy Now" ad won't interest them. Your "Free Information" ad will. Repositioning your contextual ad is better press bait, as well as prospect bait.

Getting Leads

Want to improve the success of your contextual ad campaign? Get ad viewers to subscribe to your e-mail list (or news feed). This is critical.

When people click your ad and go to your landing page, you could give them the promised free information and then make them opt into your e-mail list to get something even better. Or you could require their contact information before they get the free information (the *squeeze page* approach, see Chapter 6). There are other options, too. Most importantly, persuade them to opt into receiving communication from you before they leave.

By communicating with them on an ongoing basis, you ensure that these information searchers can become customers when the time is right for them. Or they can contact you when you're right for a story they're working on, if they're journalists.

You can reach valuable future contacts through contextual advertising. Getting them to opt into your community is essential when you're paying for clicks. After all, you've already paid to get them to your site.

> ✦ *Tip:* *Here's an insider's tip for contextual advertising, or any Internet advertising campaign really.*
>
> *When you're paying on a CPM (cost per thousand impressions) basis, drive as many people to your site as possible because you're paying every time your ad is shown anyway. Giveaways are great. Giving away free, high-quality information helps build your status as an industry expert, too.*

> *When you're paying on a PPC (pay-per-click) basis, be careful with free offers. An overly appetizing offer that attracts people who never do business with you is not profitable. Free offers generate a ton of traffic. But that traffic skyrockets your cost, too. Because it often takes longer for contextual ads to turn searchers into customers, get them to opt into receiving communication from you.*

Contextual ad viewers tend to be in research mode, not shopping mode. Therefore, aim to generate leads (or reinforce your brand). Don't push a hard sales pitch.

I know there are skeptics out there. You might be thinking, "But my 'BUY NOW!' copy works great." That could be true. There are always exceptions to general marketing guidelines. Business professionals don't all share the same business model or marketing goals, either. To improve your advertising performance, test your ads—you hold the key to your success.

Insider Insights: John Battelle

John Battelle (http://federatedmedia.net) is chairman of Federated Media Publishing and author of the bestselling book The Search.

Photo: Bart Nagel

What's the #1 mistake marketers make with contextual advertising?

Viewing customers as sales in a spreadsheet. Many marketers dump money into marketing and then solely focus on improving their conversions to justify their investment. That's one-dimensional kind of thinking.

What's your favorite simple but powerful tip?

Focus on creating a conversation with customers. Develop a message that will bring in new customers, keep them coming back, and turn them into loyal customers. That's thinking long-term about your business.

How has contextual advertising helped your business?

We use it to reinforce the Federated Media Publishing brand. We get a huge number of impressions, and a terrible click-through rate, which makes our cost for brand exposure almost nothing.

Direct Links vs. Tracking Links

There is a way to optimize your text ads for spiders, although it's becoming less effective. Because it's still worth doing in certain situations, let's explore it.

First, you should track your conversions from online advertising. A conversion is a completed action such as a sale, newsletter sign-up, or white paper download. If you're using an ad tracking tool, it typically assigns a unique tracking URL to each ad you want to track. Here's the problem: The tool's root domain, not yours, is usually in the tracking link. (This can be a problem with affiliate tracking URLs, too.)

For SEO purposes, it would be preferable for the tracking URL to be **www. yourcompany.com/ad=1** not **www.adtrackingtool/ad=1**. Otherwise, you won't get any link popularity points from spiders.

Unfortunately, an ad tracking URL is typically a redirect, which is a second problem. This means that once someone clicks on **www.adtrackingtool/ad=1**, it then redirects them to **www.yourcompany.com**. See how the underlying domain switched? Spiders don't like that.

You have several options:

✦ Choose an ad tracking tool, such as ConversionRuler, that can use your root domain in the tracking URLs. (You could also use your affiliate tracking software that offers direct linking.)

✦ Use a direct link in your text ad (**www.yourcompany.com**), instead of a third-party ad tracking link (**www.adtrackingtool/ad=1**). But, you won't be able to track leads or sales if you do this.

✦ Develop your own tracking solution and include direct links in your tracking URLs.

Don't get too excited yet.

You won't get link credit for doing contextual advertising through the search engines. Buying text links on major ad networks won't work either. The search engines filter "known" ad networks out of their ranking algorithm. In an effort to keep their organic results "pure," search engines will continue to find ads and filter them out as well.

David Johnson, director of sales and marketing for Position Research, has seen Google get a lot smarter at detecting paid links over the past year. (MSN and Yahoo! have a ways to go.) The Position Research team has tracked several cases where a client's PageRank score jumped as a result of paid text links, but improvements in the client's organic search rankings didn't follow (see Chapter 1 for information on Google's PageRank). David believes that uncovering how Google detects paid links from natural links will help reveal which text ads are slipping under Google's radar.

Google and other search engines aren't catching text ads on all sites. Small niche site and blogs are ideal candidates. If these are packed with content but few ads, they don't stick out as ad-publishing sites. Nonprofits are great; they're packed with content and are considered authority sites. Professional associations can be good as well.

As I mentioned in Chapter 1, get links from sites and blogs with content that is relevant to yours. A tax accountant should get a link from The National Association of Tax Professionals. A link from his kid's blog about Harry Potter won't help. Well, it can temporarily, but I, and other "white hat" SEO marketers, don't advise a "quantity over quality" linking strategy.

And remember, your link must be on a Web page that spiders can see. If it's behind a password-protected area, or behind a form that must be filled out, it doesn't exist. Not to spiders.

Using spider-friendly URLs, on spider-accessible Web pages, can give your text ad campaigns more power than you may have realized.

Speaking of performance, some contextual ads will tank. Not because of your copy. It's where and how ads are distributed that could not only blow your budget, but also damage your online reputation.

From Bad to Ugly

Contextual advertising is not complete without a discussion about the dark side. Yes, there is one. You need to be aware of what happens when contextual advertising goes bad, because as an advertiser, your brand is at risk.

The bad side of contextual advertising results in the inappropriate placement of your ad on publishers' Web pages. As I mentioned earlier, a tax accounting firm's ad could appear on an "I hate taxes" Web page. This is inappropriate, but not overly concerning.

However, there are stories of worse ad-matching mishaps. Business ads have appeared next to articles about a sex scandal or someone's death, for example. Although the ad-serving technology is improving, it's not perfect.

Consider using networks that show you the publishers in their network, or at least give you some degree of control over where your ad is placed. That's a simple start.

If you want to advertise in a particular network anyway, the referral data of your Web analytics reports could show you which Web pages are sending you traffic. Report inappropriate publishers to the contextual ad network provider. Hopefully, those publishers will be removed promptly.

Beware of Adware

While you're checking out contextual ad networks, find out how they distribute contextual ads. Some companies might not use publishers at all. They might use *adware*, advertising that is integrated with free applications, such as software.

For example, the software could be a toolbar or an electronic wallet. For use of the free application, users are shown ads. Sometimes, these ads are pop-ups, which annoy a great many people.

Although I won't name specific companies, several are in the center of this controversial form of advertising—especially when it's not clear to their users that adware is being installed.

Because I don't recommend this kind of contextual advertising to my clients, I can't report on any advantages. Years ago, a colleague said adware ads were quite profitable. If you go this route, investigate the online reputation of potential vendors first. (Look up the company's name and product/service names on the Web.) If you hire a company that burns unsuspecting consumers, they'll unleash their fury against your company through social media.

Spyware is a bigger problem for advertisers. This is where contextual advertising gets ugly.

Stay Away from Spyware

Spyware (also affectionately called *scumware* for obvious reasons) is similar to adware in that it can monitor Internet users' behavior to serve them ads. (Spyware can be used to spy on users and steal their personal information, too.)

But spyware is secretly bundled with free applications; users don't know that it has been installed on their computers. Worse, sometimes spyware-removing tools can't get rid of it. No ethical business professional would think spyware advertising was a good idea.

That's not the issue. The problem is that advertisers might not realize their ads are being served this way. The company that says it offers opt-in adware could actually be infecting users with spyware instead. I accidentally caught such a company while researching a story idea for *Entrepreneur* magazine.

A salesperson for the company said that people download the company's free toolbar and opt into receiving ads. Okay, so far. Then my jaw hit the floor. The salesperson mistakenly read an internal memo to me that said people who download the toolbar also receive over ten additional helpful applications. What the heck? That ain't right.

After the call, I returned to the company's Web site and noticed no adware disclosure note. The download link was even deceiving. It said something like "Click here to get started" without telling you that by clicking the link you'd download the toolbar...and ads along with it. Total scumware. This is the ugly side of contextual advertising. The moral of this story: *Be careful with whom you advertise.*

Not all contextual ad companies are evil, of course. Just do your research before giving a company your money.

Let's get back to the positive side of contextual advertising. Have you heard about people making money simply by hosting ads on their sites? They're contextual ad publishers. Becoming one can be an easy way for you to create extra, passive income.

Profiting as a Publisher

In the early days of contextual advertising, to become an ad publisher in a network, your site had to get hundreds of thousands, maybe over one million, visits a month. Obviously, only traffic powerhouses could play. Luckily, the rules have changed. Site quality, not just traffic quantity, grants you access into this community.

Contextual ad companies such as ContextWeb, IndustryBrains, Quigo, and Vibrant Media offer publishing programs, as well as advertising programs. Several still require a lot of traffic, though.

The search engines offer ad publishing programs that just about anyone can join. Google AdSense and the Yahoo! Publisher Network are two popular programs.

Set-Up Basics

Here are the basics of becoming a contextual ad publisher. Once you sign up, you'll get a piece of HTML code to put into the Web pages on which you want ads to appear. This allows ads to automatically appear on these pages. You'll be paid for clicks on those ads (or possibly for impressions, the number of times ads are shown). The ad program essentially gives you a commission from the fees the advertisers pay them. That's it!

The set-up process takes mere minutes. Well, longer if you're putting code into a lot of Web pages. If the ad publishing program lets you filter out competitors, do this. By adding your competitors' URLs to the ad filter, you'll prevent their ads from appearing on your site or blog. You certainly don't want to promote them!

Be sure to test the appearance of the ads on your Web pages. As you'll read in Entrepreneur Media's "Success Story," reviewing the ads helps you catch a competitor's ad that you may have forgotten to block.

Also try out the program's ad customization features. These can help you make more money. For example, Google AdSense offers you over 200 colors, 24 preset color palettes, and the ability to create custom color palettes to complement your site. Color is one factor that can impact the number of clicks on ads.

Publishing Google AdSense ads on your blog is a breeze. That is, if you use Blogger, Google's free blog publishing tool. From within your Blogger account, you'll choose the AdSense option from the navigation menu, and then presto! Ads appear on your blog. No touching of HTML code required. Unfortunately, even though you have a few ad formats to choose from, you can't move the ads around on your blog through the pull-down menu. Once selected, these appear under the main header of your blog. Maybe that will change by the time this book is out.

Although I've used Google AdSense as my example, check out other programs, such as the ones I mentioned earlier. Publishers are wanted! To lure Google AdSense publishers, or to attract first-time ad publishers, other programs should be making an appetizing commission offer.

If you're already an ad publisher, read programs' terms and conditions to see if you are permitted to join multiple programs. You don't want to lose a profitable revenue stream unexpectedly because you didn't read their policies. However, if you can join more than one, why not?

PPC Arbitrage

Talking about money, there's a controversial topic you need to know about: *arbitrage.*

This refers to taking advantage of two markets to earn a profit. *PPC arbitrage* usually refers to pay-per-click advertisers who bid on lower-cost keywords to drive traffic to a Web page on which they publish ads that have a higher payout (or an affiliate program that does).

Let's say an arbitrageur bids on keywords that cost an average of 10 cents a click. People click these ads and go the arbitrageur's site. He makes 25 cents a click when people click the ads on his site. This example might not seem exciting. However, there are arbitrageurs who make well over $10,000 a month.

Arbitrage is pure profit. Because PPC arbitrageurs don't sell a product or service, they don't have the headaches a business professional does. Sounds like a nice life, doesn't it?

Don't ditch your company to become a PPC arbitrageur. This isn't the magic bullet to become an overnight millionaire. Successful arbitrageurs invest time perfecting their keyword lists and creating quality content sites or blogs. Not all do, of course. Here's where the controversy heats up.

Many marketers feel arbitrage creates a poor user experience that will eventually make PPC less effective. Not all arbitrage. A quality, content-rich site or blog with ads usually escapes the controversy. It's the "ads-only" page that is under attack. As a search engine user, do you want to click a PPC ad only to land on another page full of ads? I didn't think so.

The search engines require that PPC advertisers use landing pages with quality content that provides a good user experience. You might think that ads-only landing pages would be rejected then. They're not.

Because the search engines always talk about providing a good user experience, perhaps they should require ads-only arbitrageurs to use the following in their ad copy: "Click here to see more ads." Shouldn't consumers be informed about what they'll see, instead of being tricked to click?

The topic of arbitrage is more complex than what I've shared here. As a PPC advertiser you need to be aware of it because your competitors can include arbitrageurs.

continues on page 170

Success Story
Entrepreneur Media, Inc.

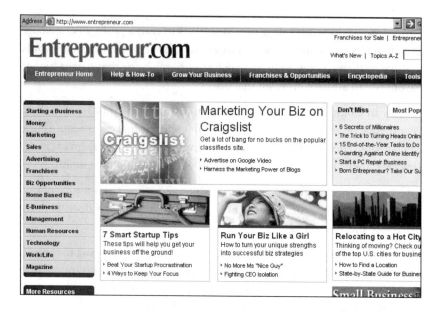

URL: www.Entrepreneur.com

Contact: Chuck Fuller

Title: Senior VP of Business Development

✦ Goals/Challenges

What were your goals for being a contextual advertising publisher?

We had two main goals. First, we wanted to serve the needs of advertisers with smaller budgets, as well as advertisers who want instant visibility and PPC pricing. We have limited ad space available through our CPM model, and the impressions we do have available are sold in advance. Our second goal was to easily create additional, passive income for Entrepreneur Media so we could continue to offer our online content for free.

What challenges/concerns did you face implementing the campaign?

Our biggest concern was being able to control parameters, such as the number of ads that appear on each page. Thanks to their customization options, we chose

Vibrant Media to provide the ads within our articles, and Business.com for the ads on the right-hand side of our content pages. Then our challenge was figuring out what parameters we needed.

✦ Strategy

Describe your implementation strategy.

Fortunately for us, the pages on our site are driven by a few core templates. In terms of implementing Vibrant Media, we only needed to put the ad-serving script within one template. However, due to the way Business.com serves their ads, we needed to place their scripts, which had been configured for specific topics, within those channels for which they were most relevant so we could serve ads that were contextually relevant.

How long did it take to launch your campaign?

It took less than one hour to post the ad-serving script on one page. And about one week to finalize our initial competitor suppression list and to test multiple pages to ensure the ads looked good and worked correctly.

What problems or surprises did you encounter, and how did you resolve them?

Occasionally, competitors appeared in the contextual ads, so we added them to our suppression list. We still scan the ads for our competitors who pop up from time to time.

✦ Results

What results did you achieve?

Within 30 days, the two contextual advertising programs boosted our gross online advertising revenue by 2 to 3 percent. Within six months, and with little effort on our part, these generated 8 to 12 percent of our gross online advertising revenue.

What's your #1 recommendation for contextual advertising publishers?

Place a limited number of contextual ads on more pages of your site. After running a few tests, we're currently limiting our ads to six within an article and five on the right-hand side. Serve your visitors with great editorial first, or they'll leave your site, never clicking those ads anyway. Adding a "resources" area on your site would be a perfect place to offer contextual ads.

continues from page 167
For example, consider changing your PPC ad copy to show that you actually sell the products or services your ad says you do. And if you see arbitrage you feel is creating a poor user experience, report this to the search engines.

If you want to host ads on your company's site or blog, you could engage in PPC arbitrage to boost your ad-publishing profits. As long as you don't distract people from doing business with you, if that's your primary goal, then becoming an ad publisher can be an instant way of generating additional revenue. The "Success Story" from Entrepreneur Media serves as a powerful example of how companies can profit quickly from their existing traffic.

Tips to Remember

For instant and massive Web exposure, try contextual advertising. Look for programs that offer transparency to help you reach, and pay for, a quality audience.

Then write ads that appeal to an information-seeking audience. If you're wondering what kind of information to offer, think about something that'll interest the press as well as prospects. Regardless of the action you want people to take when they land on your site or blog, also persuade them to opt into receiving additional information from you.

When you're ready to maximize your traffic, jump into the ad publishing side, as long as the ads you promote don't drive prospects away from your business.

You now know numerous ways to reach prospects, press, and spiders. But wait! If you sell products, there's more. Don't close this book until you read how online shopping communities can help you grow your business.

10

Targeting Shopping Communities

In many of your online marketing campaigns, your goal is to move people from *research mode* to *buy mode*. That's because Internet users are often reading online articles, press releases, blogs, e-mail, or other online content when they see your marketing message. You must be very persuasive to get them to take action. Why not take the easy road?

If you're selling products, then by advertising within online shopping communities you can connect with people who are actually shopping, not simply researching.

In the first edition of my book, *Search Engine Advertising*, I classified specialized search engines into a few categories, including comparison shopping engines and vertical market search engines.

I referenced sites such as Yahoo! Shopping, Shopping.com, MSN Shopping, BizRate, NexTag, PriceGrabber.com, and Froogle as being among the popular U.S. comparison-shopping engines. As international examples, Kelkoo is important for Europe and Alibaba for China. These engines allow shoppers to compare products and prices quickly. An SEO consultant or agency can help you submit your products to comparison-shopping engines.

In my book, I also described vertical market search engines as topic-oriented content sites with an on-site search engine. Although I included Amazon.com, eBay, and the National Gardening Association as examples of vertical market search engines, I don't think that's accurate anymore.

The National Gardening Association works here, but Amazon.com and eBay don't. Amazon.com has expanded from an online bookstore to "Online Shopping for Electronics, Apparel, Computers, Books, DVDs & more." And eBay isn't a content site with a specific topic focus—eBay is all about shopping. What was I thinking? Well, I'll tell you.

When I wrote my previous book, my colleagues and research analyst companies usually grouped the comparison shopping engines together. Other shopping sites like Amazon.com and eBay were excluded. I grouped them under the vertical market search engines, but they don't belong there.

You know, shopping engines and shopping sites seem awfully similar these days. Even though there are differences between them, they may as well be grouped together. I've even recently spotted a few agencies that now offer to manage your business on eBay, along with the shopping engines I previously mentioned. Amazon.com will no doubt be included soon, too. But are sites like eBay and Amazon.com, as well as the sites we call comparison-shopping engines, really just search engines? No.

Besides shopping, shoppers write product and merchant reviews for the entire community to see. With customers playing a key role as critics, aren't these sites shopping communities?

A community invites participation from members. That's what most, if not all, of these comparison shopping engines have in common—an active community of users. And communities like eBay take this concept one step further by creating an online space for buyers and sellers to communicate with each other via discussion boards, chat rooms, and blogs.

Even though it's time to evolve the name from "comparison shopping engines" to "online shopping communities," it's doubtful that an entire marketing industry will make the switch. That's okay.

"Community" is an important concept for you to understand as a merchant. Because even though these shopping communities share some similarities with general search engines such as Ask.com, Google, MSN Search, and Yahoo!, they're not the same.

That's why in this chapter, I'll reveal the key features of online shopping communities and how you can leverage this marketing strategy to win new customers as well as influence search engine spiders and the press.

Selling in a Community

To promote your products in online shopping communities, you'll write a listing for each product. This typically includes a product title, description, images, pricing, and shipping details. It's easy for non-techie business professionals to create a product listing in a matter of minutes.

You would, however, waste your valuable time writing listings for hundreds or thousand of products. In this case, ask your marketing agency or in-house team to create a *data feed*, which acts as a bridge between your product database and the database of the shopping community (companies such as Marketworks can help). The data feed is usually a spreadsheet or text file. Get the data feed specifications from each shopping community first because the requirements can vary.

General Costs

Let's talk about general costs.

Although it's currently free to submit your products to Froogle (via Google Base), a majority of online shopping communities charge you a small monthly subscription fee, per listing fee, pay-per-click fee, or another kind of fee for placing your products in their environments.

When shoppers click a "buy" link, they might be redirected from the shopping community to your Web site. Shopping.com and BizRate work this way. Or when shoppers click a "buy" link, they might buy your product while staying within the shopping community. Amazon.com and eBay work this way.

Start by selling a couple of items in one shopping community. When you're ready, consider upgrading to a full store, if that option is available. A store is a customizable Web site that will live inside the shopping community. Although you'll pay a little more to have a store, you'll get three big benefits: branding, organizational tools, and organic search engine traffic.

Benefits of Community Stores

Let me address the first benefit, which is branding.

When you have a store within a shopping community, you can customize it with your company logo, description, and product category names.

Plus, you can assign your individual product listings to product categories that you create within your store. This is important because when shoppers find one of your item listings, then without even leaving the shopping community, they can click to your store to learn more about your company and the other products you sell. That's great for branding, as well as sales.

A second benefit of creating a store within a shopping community is the organizational tools you get.

For example, as an eBay Store owner, you get tools to easily manage, promote, and track your business within eBay. Take advantage of them. You'll save a lot of time, and you'll be more effective. As you'll read in this chapter's "Success Story," better organizational tools and organic search engine traffic were two major reasons why Jody Rogers, vice president of Beachcombers Bazaar, upgraded from individual listings to a store on eBay.

On the topic of free search engine traffic, this is a third benefit of creating a store within a shopping community.

Actually, your individual product listings might get traffic from the organic search results, but stores are better. I'll explain why.

The online shopping communities often optimize their product category pages for the general search engines. (A community's category page could show dozens of individual product listings from various companies.) If your product listing is featured on this page, then you'll benefit from the SEO efforts of the shopping community. Unfortunately, your competitors are listed there, too. Want all eyes on your business?

Build your own store inside an online shopping community. You'll get double visibility in the general search engines. That's because both your store (within a shopping community) and Web site (outside the shopping community) can appear in top rankings; they're separate sites.

Online shopping communities, such as eBay, are making impressive strides to make their merchants' stores spider-friendly. To attract and keep profitable merchants, communities are investing big bucks into search engine optimization and pay-per-click to drive qualified traffic to merchants' stores. Why not benefit from their marketing dollars? You can piggyback off their investment while getting new customers.

In the next section, I'll reveal tips for leveraging an online shopping community's search marketing strategy to your advantage. Don't head there yet.

Regardless of whether you promote a few products or create a full store, listing your products in an online shopping community is only half of the process. To catch the attention of these shoppers and effectively compete with a growing number of merchants, you need to advertise within that community. Listing your products in an online shopping community is similar to having a site on the Web. Without marketing, nobody knows your business exists.

See, shoppers use the online shopping community's search engine, or categories, to find relevant products. Do you want your product at the bottom of the list? Of course not. Thanks again to the popularity of the pay-per-click model, many online shopping communities allow merchants to buy their way to the top. Featured advertisers get the visibility. Products at the bottom of the list don't.

Don't be frustrated by this—use it to your advantage. In fact, let's dive into the details now. Hopefully, you'll see online shopping communities in a new light.

The Smart Strategy for Search

As I just mentioned, an online shopping community might offer a pay-per-click (PPC) program that gives your products greater exposure within that community. That's not all.

You'll probably pay less per click through online shopping communities than through general search engines that offer PPC programs such as Google, MSN Search, and Yahoo!—significantly less.

Overall, fewer merchants are competing over keywords within shopping communities than on search engines. That means PPC bids aren't as high. Advertisers who can no longer afford PPC on search engines can reap a nice profit by doing PPC within shopping communities instead.

Unfortunately, your sales volume might not be as high from online shopping communities because their traffic doesn't compare yet to the high traffic of general search engines. However, your profit margins could be substantially higher.

Could it be that shopping community shoppers are ready to buy? Yup. Could it be that by paying less per click, you keep greater profits in your pockets? Yup. Too bad competition in online shopping communities is intensifying.

During an interview about doing PPC within online shopping communities, a business owner told me he watched his profits slip over a year's timeframe as he noticed new merchants jumping into his category. Like I said earlier, early adopters of new technology get rock bottom prices. It's tough to tread where few marketers have gone before, but the payoff is often worth the risk. Your competitors will catch up soon enough. Be on guard, though, because they might not be who you think they are.

Online shopping communities pose the same threat, or advantage, as affiliates when it comes to search engine advertising. Most of them are doing it. Should you bid on the same keywords they are?

Increasing Your PPC Profits

Quite frankly, if online shopping communities are bidding on generic keywords and not on your brand keywords (like trademarks), let 'em. You can't stop them anyway. What you could do is stop bidding on expensive keywords on the general search engines. Let online shopping communities pay the big bucks to attract shoppers. You bid on the categories or keywords within shopping communities to swoop up shoppers who come in. This is often a profitable PPC strategy.

Because Internet marketing programs like pay-per-click aren't new, business professionals must find ways to maximize their profits in an increasingly competitive space.

Another way to increase your PPC profits is to create a channel conflict policy about trademark marketing. As you read in Chapter 7, channel conflict refers to competing with your partners in the same space.

At some point, you'll probably notice that your marketing partners are bidding on your trademarks through PPC. Hey…you might not want that. Why should you bid against online shopping communities, your affiliates, or anyone else you consider a marketing partner, for keywords associated with your brand? These convert at an amazingly profitable rate.

In an effort to drive qualified traffic to your product listings, online shopping communities are bidding on trademarks. If you're one of their merchants, ask them to stop. Then again, you might not care. Or maybe you're letting your marketing partners do your search engine marketing for you. That's okay, too. My point is, you had better know what your channel conflict policy is, or you could be wasting money marketing against your own partners.

Maximizing Your SEO Potential

SEO is an entirely different game. Unlike other marketing partners such as some affiliates, online shopping communities won't rip off your Web site content to optimize it for the general search engines. No need to worry about a duplicate content spam violation. Remember, this is a concern if you allow your marketing partners to do SEO. (See Chapter 7 for more on this.)

In online shopping communities, you control the content for your store and product listings. So, write copy that's significantly different from your own site to avoid being penalized for duplicate content. That's how to get two listings in the general search engines.

Won't you be thrilled if your Web site *and* your store occupy two of top ten rankings? On a search results page that shows ten organic listings, you'll block two competitors from appearing if you have two sites that appear there.

This is an SEO strategy few business professionals realize. Not that I advise becoming a merchant in an online shopping community exclusively for the SEO benefit. However, as with every Internet marketing strategy I've covered in this book, whenever you can work the SEO angle into your strategy, go for it.

Ready to learn essential optimization tips?

Optimization Tips

Let's start with an individual product listing.

Use relevant keywords in your title and description. Be sure to include product details wherever possible. For example, a digital camera product listing should include the camera's brand name, model name, camera resolution, memory types, dimensions, other key features, and maybe even a product ID number.

Whoa. A lot of detail, right? This is where your keyword research comes in handy. Use the keyword tools I mentioned in Chapter 1 to discover the amazing amount of detail people use when searching for product in search engines.

When you create a store inside an online shopping community, you've got even more content to optimize for the general search engines.

I'm going to use eBay as my example again because when I joined eBay University's instructor team in 2005, I learned SEO tips from the company's Internet marketing team and from eBay expert and fellow eBay University instructor Janelle Elms.

With an eBay Store, you can use keywords in your store name (which becomes your store's URL), meta tags, description, and category names.

And Janelle let me in on a secret she said I could share with you: *Optimize your "About the Seller" page.* This is the page that describes your business. Sprinkle in relevant keywords here because by writing a content-rich page, it will tend to rank well in the organic search results.

If online shopping communities let you create a store within their network, keep these eBay Store SEO tips in mind because these may work for those, too.

Search engine marketing is critical for attracting new customers, as well as media coverage. Want a shot at instant fame? Most business professionals don't realize that an online shopping community can be a powerful public relations tool. It's the community members who ignite interest in your story and get the media to publicize it.

A Shot at Fame

Have you heard the story of Larry Star? The wedding dress guy? His auction listing on eBay catapulted him to instant celebrity status.

In April 2004, he posted a listing auctioning off his ex-wife's wedding dress. That's nothing special, right? Well, Larry's copy and photos are what ignited a PR wildfire.

In his 500-word plus description, he told his tale of wanting to burn his ex-wife's wedding dress he found in the attic. But his sister convinced him to sell it on eBay to some lucky bride-to-be. Larry also wrote that he hoped to make enough money for a couple of Seattle Mariners baseball tickets and some beer. You gotta love that. Wait, it gets better. The photos of him posing in the wedding dress steal the show. (According to his listing, he blackened out his face to prevent bar buddies and co-workers from finding out about it.) Too bad it's too long to reprint the entire listing here, but here's a short clip:

"...Actually I didn't think my head would fit in the neck hole, but then I figured if she got her Texas cheerleader hair through there I could get my head in it. Though, after looking at the pictures, I thought it made me look fat. How do you women wear this crap? I only had to walk 3 feet and I tripped twice. Don't worry ladies—I am wearing clothes on underneath it. I gotta say it did make me feel very pretty. So if it can make me feel pretty, it can make you feel pretty, especially on the most important day of your life, right?"

Um, not necessarily the item description you'd expect to see in an online shopping community, right? Larry turned his ad into a story. The result?

His listing, which has received over 17 million hits, landed him a spot on the Today Show, MSNBC's Countdown, CNBC, TLC's Wild Weddings, and a host of other television, radio, and published stories. Wow! All that press from one single item listing. At eBay Live! 2004, I spotted Larry strolling around in the famous dress with cameras flashing all around him. (He ended up keeping the dress because, apparently, the winning bidder never paid anyway.)

When Opportunity Knocks

This is a story of a guy who became a superstar sensation, thanks to online advertising. Larry capitalized on his publicity and now has his own Web site and blog (on which he publishes ads), a book entitled *Bitter, Party of One... Your Table is Ready*, and other moneymaking projects in the works. This story has a unique twist: Internet advertising helped him create a new business, not promote an existing one.

Larry Star's approach to creating his eBay listing won't work for all business professionals. Many corporate marketers won't mimic his blunt communication style. That's understandable. Someone else's marketing approach shouldn't necessarily be yours. Find your own voice.

What this story does show is how powerful of a PR tool online shopping communities can be. How can you attract the press? An entertaining product listing isn't your only option.

For example, you could auction off an item on eBay and donate part, or all, of the final sale amount to a charity (through eBay's Giving Works program). You could launch an online PR and advertising campaign promoting your charity auction, which would generate brand awareness for your company, too. And your company could win a starring role in a journalist's story. That's powerful. What could be better than building your business while also supporting nonprofit organizations? Online shopping communities like eBay give you this opportunity.

Accidental Marketing

Don't get stuck thinking eBay is the only player around. It's certainly one of the largest and most well known. Because it's the online shopping community I know best, I'm sharing several examples about it. Wait! I do have a different example. It's my personal experience as a reviewer on Amazon.com. I call this story "accidental marketing."

A few years ago, someone contacted me about my marketing services and referenced my great music review on Amazon.com in his e-mail message. That's weird, I thought. How did he see that? With a little research, I discovered something interesting.

I looked up my name in Google. (It's often called "Googling" and used as a verb as in "Hey, I Googled you!" Last summer, I watched Googling become a form of entertainment at a barbeque for writers. It was surreal. No, I didn't instigate the Googling, but I did participate.) One of my Amazon.com music reviews appeared in a top organic ranking in Google. How unexpected. Surprised, I raced to my review to make sure I didn't say anything inappropriate. Whew. Then a light bulb appeared over my head: An online customer review can get visibility in the organic search results...even if it's by accident.

That said, write your customer reviews assuming spiders will find them and expose them to the entire Web world. But don't turn your review into an ad. Otherwise, members will angrily complain, and your review will be immediately removed.

It's interesting to know that your product review could pop up in the search results, isn't it? This is yet another publicity opportunity, if executed right. Always write for your human audience first. Spiders will notice.

Customer reviews, posted in online shopping communities, are your biggest asset—not the reviews you post, but the ones your customers post about you.

Insider Insights: Janelle Elms

Janelle Elms (www.janelleElms.com), eBay University instructor, best-selling author, and online business consultant, who specializes in coaching people on how to build successful eBay businesses and maximize their profits.

What's the #1 mistake eBay sellers make with their buyers?

Thinking like a seller instead of a buyer. I call it the "spaghetti test"—throwing their auctions up on eBay and hoping they stick to a buyer. They should use eBay to research competitors and then create more effective listings...better title keywords, pricing strategy, and even shipping offers.

What's your favorite simple but powerful tip?

Write a description as though you don't have a photo, and take a photo as though you don't have a description.

How has eBay helped your business?

eBay has created an international marketplace that allows me to reach any customer, worldwide, who has access to a computer. My sales, on average, have gone up by almost 20 percent since offering my items internationally.

Your Customers Are Talking

Your product listings draw in prospects, but your customer reviews close the sale. If you neglect to manage these, you could suffer from a damaged brand and a loss of business.

In online shopping communities, you're only as good as your customers say you are.

When I was looking for a flat-panel LCD monitor, I asked my dad, a techie gadget guy, what kind I should buy and where I should buy it. Along with overwhelming me with more details than I wanted to know about the technology, he named a few models I should consider. Then without hesitation he sternly warned me about a merchant I should absolutely avoid. "Their reputation is

TERRIBLE!" he insisted. Then he rattled off a list of offenses, including poor customer service and not honoring rebates. How did he know that?

It turns out, he checked out customer reviews on online shopping communities. Way to go, Dad! More than a year later, I still remember that merchant. The company's bad online reputation had been burned into my skull.

This story shows how your customers are talking about you. They're posting their reviews for all in the online shopping community to see. Are you watching? Are you responding? It doesn't take too many negative reviews for your potential customers to associate a negative image with your brand. You can't afford *not* to be paying attention.

While writing this chapter, I followed up on my father's initial analysis of the "terrible" merchant. I chose a shopping community and poked around the customer reviews for that company. Sure enough, poor customer service and not honoring rebates were the two most common complaints.

To my surprise, the merchant scored high marks, too—for fast shipping and great prices. Reviews are a huge help. I might be willing to try this merchant again if fast delivery and cheap prices are my priorities. I wouldn't buy from this merchant if the great price were dependent on a rebate. A lack of customer service could be a deal breaker also.

See how your potential customers are evaluating your company? They're not just looking at price. That's good to know, isn't it? Many business professionals assume they can't effectively compete in online shopping communities because their prices are higher than other merchants' prices.

True, online shoppers love a great deal. But they want quality, too, and a merchant they can trust.

You need to routinely monitor your online customer reviews for several reasons.

✦ First, these reviews reveal the current state of your online reputation. It could be good, or you could use a makeover. Take the good stuff and use it in your marketing materials. Use the bad stuff as information for self-reflection and improvement. Basically, fix what everyone else says is broken.

✦ Second, keep an eye on your customer reviews to respond immediately to customers' negative experiences. Just as with social media, you can turn ugly publicity into shiny gold stars. Respond to unhappy customers. Once you've resolved their problem, ask them to post a review. Hopefully, they can edit their complaint. If not, they can post a new review praising your heroic efforts at resolving their problem. All better. Almost.

Who else could be posting negative reviews? Yes, your competitors.

Unfortunately, online shoppers aren't always required to be your customers to post a review. Plus, they might be able to write a review without including any of their personal information for the public to see. These things allow competitors to launch a guerilla brand-burning raid against your company. That is, if you're not paying attention.

Watch out for generic complaints like "What a horrible company!" This could be a competitor in disguise. Some online shopping communities let you post public replies to complainers. Do it. Show other shoppers you're happy to resolve your customers' problems. A simple "We want happy customers! Please call us at <phone number> so we can help you right away" might do the trick. Your response can counteract the negative review.

That's using good publicity to fight bad publicity. Also, find out if you can report inappropriate customer reviews.

A colleague of mine received a scathing book review from a competitor on Amazon.com. After she reported the obvious attack, it was removed. Next to a review on Amazon.com is a "Report This" link, which allows shoppers to report inappropriate content. Although shoppers sometimes police customer reviews, you should routinely review your own reviews. After all, it's your online reputation at stake.

Your competitors can actually help you improve your marketing strategy. Want to know why? Head to the next section and find out.

Your Competitors Are Leaking

Your competitors aren't leaking critical information about their companies in online shopping communities. But their customers are!

You can learn a lot about the strengths and weaknesses of your competitors by checking out their customer reviews. You can then use this information to strengthen your own marketing strategy.

In certain online shopping communities, you can sort customer reviews to scan quickly the best and worst of the list. In mere minutes you could discover that your competitors have stellar, or terrible, customer service. What can you do with this information?

Well, if your chief competitors outscore you in customer service, it's time to overhaul yours or bring in an expert who can help you improve your company's performance. If you don't fix what your customers consistently tell you is broken, they'll continue to write reviews that reinforce the online reputation you really don't want.

Here's the fun part.

If you notice your customer service outscores theirs, promote this competitive advantage in all of your marketing materials. You can promote your stellar customer service on your Web site, article and e-zine bylines, or even pay-per-click ads. Don't forget your offline marketing materials either. Your online reputation supports your claims.

Many shoppers, like my father, head to online shopping communities to help them make a purchasing decision. If the strengths you promote in your offline and online ads are the same strengths praised by your current customers, online shoppers should convert quickly into new customers. That is, if they see those raving customer reviews.

Feature Customer Reviews

Not all prospects head to online shopping communities. Many start with a general search engine. Or they look for online articles that compare products and merchants.

When these prospects come across a link to your Web site, they'll head straight there, never seeing your glowing ratings and reviews sitting inside online shopping communities. Unless…your site features these as testimonials.

If you've got great reviews, flaunt 'em.

Post your best reviews on your Web site and then link directly to these on the associated shopping community for verification purposes. (Remember to choose the reviews that blow away your competitors' reviews in case shoppers head to theirs next.) Launching a new, smaller Web browser window to showcase these reviews is a critical step for keeping your Web site in view.

Or promote your overall merchant rating score from several communities where you score well. You could link your score to the home page of the associated shopping community, letting your Web site visitors do their own research. But you may lose them. Again, open a new, smaller Web browser window or consider featuring your score without providing a link. You want sales, not just credibility.

As I mentioned in my first book, a customer testimonial on your site could be seen as contrived, whereas a customer review in an online shopping community has a higher degree of credibility. It hasn't been filtered by you. This doesn't mean testimonials on your site aren't valuable. They are! I'm just pointing out a special benefit of reviews posted in shopping communities. They seem more "real." Again, because those words are coming from your customers, or competitors, keep a close eye on them.

The Media Is Watching

And as I've been saying throughout this book, remember the press! With tight deadlines, journalists appreciate all the help they can get in connecting with quality consultants and companies to interview.

One way journalists evaluate the credibility of merchants is by reading their customer testimonials. Many times, there's no client list on a company's site. Or there's no "In the News" section where they can see if the company has been checked out and interviewed by other journalists.

As a journalist, if I can't get a sense of an unfamiliar company's credibility, I move on. I won't risk interviewing a company without a track record. By the time my article gets published, the company could be out of business. Happy customer reviews and testimonials can certainly contribute to a company's credibility.

Because this is an online marketing book, I couldn't weave in offline marketing campaign ideas; however, an integrated marketing strategy is essential. You can drive online traffic to offline locations, as well as use offline marketing to get online exposure.

I connected with Jody Rogers, vice president of Beachcombers Bazaar, when we were offline, not online. We chatted at eBay Live! 2005, and she handed me her business card. On the card were the keywords "Handmade Khussa, Glass Bangles, All Natural Henna, Ethnic Jewelry." And the beautiful eyes of a woman with jewelry adorning her forehead caught my attention. Later, I visited her eBay Store and Web site, which all visually coordinated with each other. Great branding. This entrepreneur had it going on!

continues on page 188

Success Story
Beachcombers Bazaar

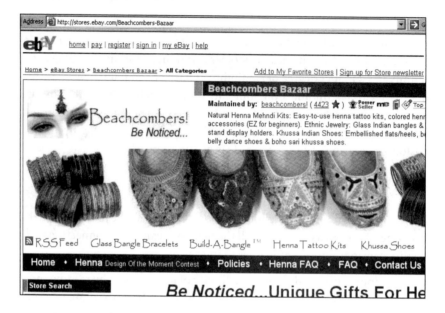

URL: http://stores.ebay.com/Beachcombers-Bazaar

Contact: Jody Rogers

Title: Vice President

✦ Goals/Challenges

What were your goals for launching an eBay Store?

We wanted to take our part-time eBay sales to a full-time business. We thought we could better organize our products, give buyers a destination, have a permanent eBay and search engine presence, develop our brand, and cross-promote products.

What challenges/concerns did you face implementing the campaign?

We knew nothing about HTML, branding, marketing, or SEO. We stumbled through the beginning and educated ourselves with books, eBay Live!, and the eBay Stores Discussion Board.

✦ Strategy

Describe your implementation strategy.

We started by creating custom categories to make shopping for our items easier, and by focusing on who we were and what we wanted our image to be. We actively created our Beachcombers! brand, learned about SEO, and applied it to our store. We made our store interactive and fun (Build-A-Bangle™, Henna Design Contest), while focusing on what we were good at: service and sales.

How long did it take to launch your eBay Store?

One day to set up and six months to move the store to something we could be proud of.

What problems or surprises did you encounter, and how did you resolve them?

We discovered how many inadvertent eBay rule violations we had. Many eBay rules are vague, contradictory, and constantly changing. This creates problems when your listings are removed or your store is closed because of a misunderstood violation. The Stores Discussion Board was a lifesaver. We found people willing to give advice and provide links to little known eBay rules. I still avidly read the Board to keep up with new information and to get ideas.

Our day-to-day activities were soon taking up too much time, and we realized automation was needed to grow. We added an auction management system, Marketworks, to automate day-to-day tasks. eBay's fee increase in 2005 made us rethink our strategy and caused us to diversify into other venues, including Overstock Auctions, Yahoo! Auctions, and our own Web site. A very good move, it turned out.

✦ Results

What results did you achieve?

We increased our average eBay sales by more than 30 percent with multiple purchases and gained a large repeat customer base. Expanding our eBay business gave us the means to expand into other successful online venues. An eBay Store is an inexpensive way to reach a huge number of potential customers.

What's your #1 recommendation for eBay Sellers?

Brand yourself. Target exactly what your business is and work it. Make yourself different and memorable. We focus on three main points: uniqueness, quality, and service. Find your points and focus your business on them.

continued from page 185
Unlike many business professionals who see online shopping communities as a later phase of Internet marketing, Jody launched her company in one. And she grew it from a part-time job to a full-time business. I wanted to feature someone who took this approach. Beachcombers Bazaar is an eBay success story. But the story doesn't end there. Since we met, Jody has expanded her Internet marketing efforts, exemplifying how business professionals should maximize their visibility through a variety of channels.

Tips to Remember

To reach ready shoppers, advertise your products within online shopping communities.

Use relevant keywords in your product listings to score additional visibility in the search engines. When you're ready, launch a store within a shopping community to optimize that additional content for the spiders, as well as get access to time-saving management tools. Then think about ways to leverage an online shopping community as a PR tool.

Continually ask customers to post reviews to help you attract new customers and score credibility points with the press. Monitor your customer reviews and respond to unhappy customers immediately because your online reputation is shaped by your customers' experiences.

Finally, to get a marketing edge on your competitors, study their reviews to find out their strengths and weaknesses. Use this information to promote your strengths in your marketing materials.

In Conclusion

Do you have an Internet marketing question, comment, or success story to share? Then stop by my site and blog at **www.CatherineSeda.com**. And be sure to get my free Top Ten Internet Marketing Mistakes report.

To your online success!

Catherine Seda

HARD WORK. DEDICATION. EATING, BREATHING
AND LIVING YOUR DREAMS, EVERY DAY. PUSHING
HARDER. TAKING RISKS WHEN OTHERS WON'T.
NEVER STOPPING. NEVER SURRENDERING. BEING
FEARLESS. BEING A LEADER. INSPIRING YOURSELF.
INSPIRING THOSE AROUND YOU. EVERY DAY.

WHAT DOES IT TAKE TO BE AN ENTREPRENEUR?

OUR READERS KNOW.

TO SUBSCRIBE
CALL 1-800-274-6229
OR VISIT US ONLINE AT
WWW.ENTREPRENEUR.COM

Stay on the cutting edge of
Internet marketing with
Catherine Seda, who has been
writing Entrepreneur
magazine's popular "Net
Sales" column since 2003.

Entrepreneur
MAGAZINE

www.entrepreneur.com I AOL Keyword: Entrepreneur

Index